Pursuing God's
Beauty

Also by Margaret Feinberg

The Organic God

The Sacred Echo:
Hearing God's Voice in Every Area of Your Life

Scouting the Divine:
My Search for God in Wine, Wool, and Wild Honey

Hungry for God:
Hearing God's Voice in the Ordinary and Everyday

Pursuing God's Love:
Stories from the Book of Genesis DVD Bible Study

SIX SESSIONS

Margaret Feinberg

Pursuing God's
Beauty

PARTICIPANT'S GUIDE

Stories from the Gospel of John

ZONDERVAN®

ZONDERVAN.com/
AUTHORTRACKER
follow your favorite authors

ZONDERVAN

Pursuing God's Beauty Participant's Guide
Copyright © 2011 by Margaret Feinberg

This title is also available as a Zondervan ebook. Visit www.zondervan.com/ebooks.

Requests for information should be addressed to:

Zondervan, *Grand Rapids, Michigan* 49530

ISBN 978-0-310-42869-5

Cover design: *Kirk DouPounce*
Cover photography: *Corbis Images*
Interior design: *Sherri Hoffman*

Printed in the United States of America

11 12 13 14 15 16 /DCI/ 25 24 23 22 21 20 19 18 17 16 15 14 13 12 11 10 9 8 7 6 5 4 3 2 1

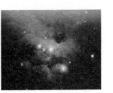

Contents

Pursuing God's Beauty

Beauty has a way of stopping us in our tracks. When we encounter something that's truly beautiful, we can't help but pause for a moment.

I've seen beautiful expressions, such as the lingering nuances of the setting sun, cause people to pause, watch, and reflect as they drink in the scene. Indeed, beauty has a way of gripping our hearts and refusing to let go.

Why pursue God's beauty?

Because the beauty of God radiates in the person of Jesus Christ — the person in whom God placed his whole heart on display for the world to see.

The Gospel of John is a book whose beauty invites us to stop in our tracks, not just because it's beautifully written, but because of the stunning portraits of Jesus found throughout. The twenty-one chapters of John tell stories of Jesus walking into people's lives and transforming them forever. Jesus knows no boundaries. The Son of God enters the lives of fishermen and centurions, the physically and spiritually blind, as well as a wide range of religious leaders and religious rejects, inviting them all to believe. Those who accept the invitation find their lives forever changed.

Despite the overwhelming presence of God's beauty, some are tempted to dismiss beauty as merely subjective because aesthetic opinions differ. Others dismiss beauty as deceptive because some have perverted beauty into unmentionables. Still others turn away from beauty because it's not essential or functional.

Yet God is the one who fills all of creation with beauty. God strings galaxies in the sky and submerges creatures in the depths of the sea — some of which have yet to be discovered. Indeed, the heavens and earth declare the glory of God. The stories found in John are ones we need to study and be reminded of because they beckon us to love God even more.

My hope and prayer is that through this study you'll be reminded of the work of God in your life and share that beautiful news with others.

Blessings,
Margaret

A Message for Leaders

The six sessions of *Pursuing God's Beauty* are designed to be accessible for people to grow in their knowledge of God and Scripture. Whether participants are still trying to figure out who God is or made the decision to follow Jesus decades ago, you'll find material that reaches them wherever they are in their spiritual journey.

Here are a few guidelines to help you and your group get the most out of this study.

Tailor the Study to Your Group

Groups are as diverse as the unique people in them. Some groups will want to watch one DVD session each week and complete the study in six weeks. Others may want to focus on the DVD one week and continue the discussion the next, creating a twelve-week study. Some groups will want to watch the DVD and then discuss as a large group; others will prefer to watch the DVD together and then break into smaller groups to discuss. Tailor the study to what best suits your group.

Select an Experiential Activity or Icebreaker Question in Advance

Each group session offers two options for getting started: an Experiential Activity or a selection of Icebreaker Questions. If your gathering is an hour or less, you may want to skip the activity or icebreaker question and dive right into the DVD so you have plenty of time for discussion. If your gathering is longer than an hour, select either the activity or one of the questions for your group.

Before the first meeting, read through all the experiential activities in the study. Select the ones you'd like to do and make a list of items you need to purchase, gather, or research. For example, if you want to buy some nard for lesson four, order it now so it arrives in plenty of time.

Consider inviting a handful of participants to organize the experiential activity each week. This will encourage involvement and develop leadership skills of the participants.

Select Discussion Questions in Advance

Each session includes a variety of discussion questions. Some questions focus on encouraging people to open up about their lives and others focus more on wrestling with Scripture and the material presented on the DVD.

More questions are provided than time will allow for most groups—don't feel like you have to ask every question. Before you gather, highlight the questions you want to focus on during the session. Select the questions best suited to the interests and objectives of your group. You may even want to develop a few questions of your own.

As you lead the discussion, remember that silence can be a friend. You may ask a question and be greeted with silence. Allow the silence to rest for a moment and see who speaks up. If you have a participant who is particularly quiet and you're asking an open-ended question that anyone could answer, consider calling on that person by name. Gently ask, "What do you think, Josh?" Try to avoid questions that lead to "yes" and "no" answers, and stay focused on learning more about God and deepening relationships.

Throughout the study, you'll discover quotes, scholarly observations, and various insights. Invite discussion on the content of these boxes and see what develops.

Encourage Participants to Engage in Afterhours Studies (If They Can)

Each session includes five Afterhours personal studies. The goal of Afterhours is to challenge participants to keep diving deeper into the Gospel of John. Encourage participants to engage in the personal studies, but remember that not everyone will be able to do so. Remind participants that even if they aren't able to do Afterhours, they're still welcome to be part of the study. If they can only do one personal study each week, encourage them to complete Day Five, which specifically prepares participants for the next group session.

Stay Connected

Encourage participants to connect with Margaret on her website at *www.margaretfeinberg.com*, via Twitter @mafeinberg, or "like" her on Facebook. If you get a chance, take a photo of your group and it could be posted on her website. Email your photo to *info@margaretfeinberg.com* and include the name of your church or group.

Encountering Jesus
John 1–3

> Each one of us has different experiences of God's beauty and different appreciations of this beauty — those inexpressible and indefinable moments that deeply touch our hearts, our minds, and all our senses. Those moments that melt our hearts when we feel the presence of God in what is beautiful. Each one of us will tell different stories of when we have heard beauty, seen beauty, smelled beauty, tasted beauty and touched beauty ... when beauty has touched our inner souls, when God has touched us.[1]
>
> —*Edward F. Markquart*

Throughout the Gospel of John, the beauty of God radiates in the person of Jesus Christ—a person in whom God placed his whole heart on display for the world to see. It's within the person of Jesus that we find the invisible attributes of God being made visible, on display like the fine pieces of artwork in a gallery—to be enjoyed, celebrated, and reflected upon.

If we are going to be people who pursue God's beauty, who live passionately pursuing Jesus Christ, then we cannot keep the stories of what God has been doing in our lives to ourselves. Each of us is a mini-portrait of the beautiful work of God. As recipients of God's grace and love, we have the opportunity to display the beauty of God everywhere we go simply by sharing the story of God's work in our lives.

Wherever we may be on our spiritual journeys, there's something powerful and beautiful we can discover from each other's stories of meeting Jesus. Every story showcases facets of God's goodness and demonstrates how relentlessly God pursues us.

Getting Started: Select One

Experiential Activity: When Love Comes to Town

What you'll need:

- ◆ An MP3 of U2's "When Love Comes to Town"
- ◆ Printed lyrics of U2's "When Love Comes to Town" for each participant

1. Download "When Love Comes to Town."
2. Google the lyrics and print them out for each participant.
3. Play the song and allow participants to read through the lyrics.
4. Discuss the following questions:

   - What images and messages are suggested through the song?
   - What does it look like in your own life when love comes to town?
   - Have you ever seen love come to town in someone else's life? What did it look like? How were they transformed? How were you impacted from seeing the transformation?

Icebreaker Question

If you're not doing the experiential activity, choose one *of the following sets of questions to begin your discussion.*

- Where did you notice beauty this week? How did it impact your relationship with God?
- Have you ever met someone famous? Describe the experience.
- Imagine for a moment that you had the opportunity to meet Jesus tomorrow morning for breakfast at a local restaurant. Where would you eat together? What would you order? What questions would you ask?

One: Encountering Jesus

(18 MINUTES)

As you watch the DVD, use the following outline to take notes on anything that stands out to you.

We all have different stories, unique portraits of the ways we first encountered Jesus.

At times we will simply declare the truth of who Jesus is, and those who hear will become followers of Jesus.

We need to bring people to Jesus. What does that mean? We need to recognize that bringing people to Jesus is a journey in which we share our faith and our lives.

Sometimes when it comes to helping people encounter Jesus, all we can do is invite them to "come and see."

Sometimes people will have encounters with God that are miraculous, mysterious, beyond human explanation, but essential for their decision to follow Jesus.

If we are going to be people who pursue God's beauty, people who want to see our magnificent God on display everywhere we go, then we cannot keep the stories of what God has been doing in our lives to ourselves.

Group Discussion Questions

(30–45 MINUTES)

1. What caught your attention or stood out most to you on the DVD?

Encountering Jesus

2. How did you first encounter Jesus? Where were you? Who were you with? What series of circumstances led to that encounter?

3. Jesus' approach to calling his disciples was revolutionary. Traditionally, disciples made the choice of which rabbi they would follow. But Jesus does the opposite. Instead of waiting for the disciples to find him, Jesus takes the initiative and pursues his followers. Read John 1:35 – 50 aloud. Which of the disciples' experiences most closely resembles your own experience in deciding to follow Jesus?

When You Can't Keep the Good News to Yourself

4. Philip enthusiastically shares with Nathanael the good news that he has found the Messiah. Rather than share in the excitement, Nathanael asks whether any good thing can come out of Nazareth. The response isn't exactly what Philip hoped for!

Have you ever had someone share their faith with you? Describe your response.

Have you ever shared your faith and the response wasn't what you had hoped for? How did you handle the situation?

Notable

Jesus responds to Nathanael by acknowledging that he's an Israelite in whom there's nothing deceitful or false. The wording of the statement suggests that Nathanael is different from Jacob (before his name changed to Israel) in that he is honest and true.

5. Sometimes those who are the most cynical have the deepest hungers and desires that have gone unmet. Nathanael's response to Philip's news that he's found the Messiah is marked by cynicism.

   What are some specific situations that you've encountered in the last three months that have tempted you to respond with cynicism?

   What do you think is the best way to respond to someone with cynical views of God and Christianity?

6. Are you inviting people on a regular basis, as Philip did, to "come and see" Jesus? Why or why not?

7. What compels or hinders you from sharing your faith?

Bonus Activity

The cover of this study bears an image of "The Sword of Orion" from the constellation Orion. To learn more about this image, go online and Google images from the Hubble Telescope as well as this constellation. Thank God for the beauty of creation.

8. Are there some ways you've seen God work to draw people to himself that make you uncomfortable or quietly think, "I wish God *didn't* work that way?" If so, describe. Are there ways in which God works to draw people closer that you love to see? If so, describe.

Come and See

9. Are there any methods, techniques, or conversation starters that you've personally found effective for sharing your faith? If you were to create a "Five Best Practices" list for sharing your faith, what would you place on the list?

10. The Gospel of John is written so that people will not only encounter Jesus but believe in Jesus. Read John 20:30–31.

From this first lesson, what details, stories, or interactions would lead you to believe in Jesus?

Have you ever seen someone's life transformed in a beautiful way because they chose to believe in Jesus? If so describe.

Jesus is in the business of drawing people into a beautiful relationship with himself. We have the opportunity to share the good news of who Jesus is and all that he has done and, in the process, to bring people to Jesus so they grow in their faith and knowledge of him.

Close in Prayer

Ask God to:

- Give you courage to share your faith both in words and actions.
- Provide opportunities to introduce people to Jesus as well as sensitivity to when those moments arrive.
- Make the good news truly *good* news in your life so that it bubbles out of you.

Jumpstart

To get an insider's look at the Pursuing God series, bonus features, and freebies, as well as join the online discussion, visit *www.pursuinggodbiblestudy.com*.

To prepare for the next group session, read John 4:1–45 and tackle the After-hours personal studies.

Bonus Activity

Take a quick photo! Before you close, take a picture of your group and email it to *info@margaretfeinberg.com*. Your group could be featured soon on the home page of *www.margaretfeinberg.com*.

Afterhours Personal Studies

Dive deeper into John's Gospel by engaging in these five personal studies. If you only have time for one, choose Day Five, which will prepare you specifically for the next session.

DAY ONE: The Uniqueness of John's Gospel
John 1:1–5

All four of the Gospels tell the stories of Jesus in a unique way. Matthew provides a detailed account of Jesus' actions and interactions. Mark's Gospel is short, sweet, and gets straight to the point about Jesus. Luke is written from the perspective of a doctor and businessman. If you want to dive into the miracles of Jesus or learn more about what Jesus thinks of financial issues, study the Gospel of Luke.

Then there's John, an artist who goes beyond the facts about Jesus to communicate the personality, the emotions, the very presence of Christ in history. John's Gospel adds color and vibe and hue to the gospel story. This beautifully written account is lined with distinctive snapshots of Jesus, his teaching, and his heart for our world.

All of the Gospels help people encounter Jesus in different ways. Let's look at the distinct ways each of the four Gospels begins.

1. Read Matthew 1:1–17. As a Jewish disciple of Jesus, Matthew begins by looking at the family tree of Jesus in order to emphasize Jesus as the legitimate King of Israel. What does Matthew's introduction reveal about his purpose for writing? Make a list of three to five words that describe Matthew's writing style (for example: *logical, detailed, in-depth*).

2. Read Mark 1:1–8. Directed toward a Roman audience, Mark uses a completely different method of reaching his audience than Matthew. What does Mark's introduction reveal about his purpose for writing? Make a list of three to five words that describe Mark's writing style.

Quotable

"The essence of the depth of John's picture of Jesus is its simplicity. Light, water, bread, seed sown. Jesus is revealed through the immediate, the tangible. He left out the parables of Jesus because, for John, Jesus' entire life was a parable; a parable of misunderstanding, of pain, of joy."[2]

—Michael Card

3. Read Luke 1:1–4. Unlike Matthew, Luke traces Jesus' lineage all the way to Adam. What does Luke's introduction reveal about his purpose for writing? Make a list of three to five words that describe Luke's writing style.

Notable

John was written significantly later than the other three Gospels. Thus, the author of John's Gospel would have been aware of the other Gospels (especially Mark), but pointedly chose specific instances and personal interactions with Jesus to express in his Gospel.

4. Read John 1:1–5. Instead of beginning with Adam and the first human, John begins even before then. John paints a breathtakingly beautiful portrait of the reality of God incarnate in the person of Jesus Christ. What does John's introduction reveal about his purpose for writing? Make a list of three to five words that describe John's writing style.

5. Which of these four approaches to telling the story of Jesus appeal to your own personality and learning style?

6. Why is it important to study the stories of Jesus? How has studying the stories of Jesus within the Gospels affected your faith in the past?

Spend some time asking God to whet your appetite to know God even more! Ask God to increase your hunger to study Scripture and celebrate the discoveries you make along the way.

DAY TWO: Seeing Jesus in Images, Titles, and Roles
John 1

Throughout the first chapter of John, a wide variety of images, titles, and roles are used in order to introduce readers to Jesus. Since John's Gospel is written to a diverse audience, John describes Jesus using beautiful imagery that appeals to a wide audience—Greeks, Romans, Gentiles, and Jews. Jesus came to save all of humanity, not just a particular people group.

1. Read John 1. Use the following chart to write down the images, titles, or roles John uses to describe Jesus.

Scripture	Images, titles, or roles that describe Jesus
John 1:1	*Example: Word, logos*
John 1:4	
John 1:5, 9	
John 1:14	
John 1:15	
John 1:18	
John 1:29, 36	
John 1:34	
John 1:38	
John 1:41	
John 1:45	
John 1:49	

2. Identifying Jesus as the Word (or Logos), life, and light provides a cosmic perspective of Jesus. Jesus was not only with God in the beginning, but creation did not happen apart from Jesus. Life is found in Jesus, not just through creation, but also through the reconciliation of humanity to God through the person of Jesus.

According to this chapter, what role does Jesus play in creation?

What is the significance of Jesus being incarnate — fully divine and fully human?

How do you think your relationship with God would be different if Jesus had not been fully human?

3. What do the images, titles, and roles reveal about Jesus' relationship with God? (*Hint:* See John 1:14, 15, 18, 29, 34, 36.)

4. What do the images, titles, and roles reveal about Jesus' role in relationship to the people of Israel? (*Hint:* See John 1:37, 41, 45, 49.)

5. What do the images, titles, and roles allude to regarding Jesus' future death and resurrection? (*Hint:* See John 1:29, 36.)

6. Of all the images, titles, and roles for Jesus mentioned in this chapter, which one is most beautiful and meaningful to you? And how is it significant for you right now?

Spend some time in prayer asking God to reveal Jesus to you in a fresh way. Ask God to open up the understanding of your mind and heart to comprehend and embrace the reality of Jesus in your life during the upcoming weeks.

DAY THREE: Creating and Cleansing

John 2

After introducing us to Jesus, John highlights seven miracles called "signs" which point to Jesus as the much-anticipated Messiah. The first of these signs is a somewhat startling event. Jesus unexpectedly turns water into wine for a wedding celebration. The dramatic and prophetic act is meant to demonstrate Jesus' divine power and lead the reader to believe that Jesus is the Messiah. The Greek word for the "good" wine Jesus creates is *kalos*, which can be translated "beautiful." Thus the miracle Jesus performs is creating beautiful wine.

1. Read John 2:1–12. The passage begins with the words, "On the third day." Three days seems to be significant throughout Scripture. According to the following passages, what other events happened on the third day?

Scripture	On the third day ...
Genesis 22:1–12	*Example: Abraham journeys to Mount Moriah to offer Isaac as a sacrifice. On the third day, Abraham arrives only to have an angel stop him before he can kill his son.*
Genesis 40:12–23	

Scripture	On the third day ...
Hosea 6:1 – 2	
John 2:19	
1 Corinthians 15:3 – 8	

Reflecting on these passages, what does the third day represent or symbolize to you?

Weddings in ancient culture lasted anywhere from three days to an entire week. Often the entire community — including friends and family — were involved in the celebration, placing a considerable burden on the host family. Jesus is attending a wedding in the small town of Cana in Galilee along with his disciples when his mother announces the hosts are out of wine.

Running out of wine in ancient culture meant public disgrace and shame. Jesus' brusque response to the immediate need for wine suggests he isn't overly concerned with the family's social faux pas. Rather than call his mother by her first name, he asks, "Woman, why do you involve me? My hour has not yet come." It is worth noting that throughout John's Gospel, Jesus' mother is never identified as Mary.

Mary doesn't waiver. She has no idea what her son will do, but she trusts he will do what's best. Mary tells the servants to do whatever Jesus instructs.

Jesus instructs the servants to fill six stone ceremonial jars totaling somewhere between 120 and 180 gallons with water. Then he asks that some be taken to the master of the banquet who has no idea of the sequence of events that led to the tasting. Like a sommelier, the master comments on the high quality of the wine and asks why they've saved the beautiful wine for now, when it should have been served first.

2. What does this story, the first of seven signs, reveal to you about Jesus?

What within this story persuades you that Jesus is the incarnate Word of God?

After the first sign or miracle of turning water into wine, Jesus, his mother and brothers, and the disciples travel to Capernaum. With Passover approaching, Jesus makes the first of three journeys to Jerusalem to celebrate the Passover (John 2:13; 6:4; 11:55).

Traveling to Jerusalem to celebrate a feast was not uncommon. Jews made an annual pilgrimage for three different feasts: Passover, Tabernacles, and Weeks (Pentecost). Of all of the feasts, Passover was considered the most important. The feast celebrates God's deliverance of the Jewish people from slavery in Egypt. When the death angel passed over the homes, those whose doorposts had been marked with blood had their firstborn child's life spared. (For a deeper understanding of the Passover, read Exodus 12.)

Upon arrival in the temple, Jesus encounters people selling oxen, sheep, and doves as well as exchanging money. The practices were not unusual; in fact, the pilgrims needed them. Temple practices required animals for sacrifice and it was often impractical to insist people travel long distances with their animals. In addition, the required temple tax had to be paid in the local currency. While many of the travelers probably appreciated their services, Jesus has a different response.

The focus of John's Gospel isn't to create a chronological account of Jesus' life so much as it is proclaiming the life and ministry of Christ and inviting people to believe in him. While the other Gospels feature the story of Jesus overturning the tables at the close of Jesus' ministry (Matthew 21:13; Mark 11:17; Luke 19:46), John places it at the beginning.

3. Read John 2:13–25. While salespeople and moneychangers had their place in serving the travelers to Jerusalem, they should have been conducting their business *near* the temple rather than *in* the temple. Their disregard shows contempt and irreverence for God. Instead of *helping* people worship God, their presence inside the temple *impeded* worship. How do you think onlookers responded to Jesus' reaction in the temple?

4. How does the image of Jesus in verses 15–16 compare and contrast with popular images of Jesus in our culture?

How does the image of Jesus in verses 15–16 compare and contrast with your own understanding and image of Jesus?

Following Jesus' passionate display of cleansing the temple, the disciples reflect on Psalm 69:9. Some of the Jews watching the scene unfold ask for a sign. Jesus says that if they destroy the temple, then in three days he will raise it up (John 2:19). Throughout John's Gospel, Jesus will say many things that are misunderstood or misinterpreted.

5. What do you think Jesus' cleansing of the temple as well as the promise to rebuild the temple symbolizes?

How do Jesus' statements set the stage for his death and resurrection?

6. What areas of your heart do you feel need to be cleansed? What do you think Jesus would drive out of your heart?

Spend some time asking God if there are any areas of your life in which you need to ask forgiveness and make a change. Ask God to cleanse you from the inside out.

While the wedding at Cana offered a miraculous sign of Jesus' divinity and the overturning of the tables in the temple provided a prophetic sign, John's Gospel now offers us another glimpse of Jesus and his mission.

While still in Jerusalem, Jesus is visited by Nicodemus, a wealthy member of the Sanhedrin, the Jewish ruling council composed of Sadducees and Pharisees. Since John's Gospel has already revealed Jesus as the light (John 1:5), it's no small detail that Nicodemus comes to Jesus at night and engages in a conversation that changes his life forever. The only other person to approach Jesus at night is Judas Iscariot (John 13:30).

1. Read John 3. Much speculation surrounds Nicodemus' motives and character. The fact that he visits Jesus at night suggests Nicodemus is afraid of being seen by other religious leaders. What title does Nicodemus use to address Jesus? What does this reveal about Nicodemus' attitude and respect toward Jesus? (*Hint:* See John 3:2.)

2. What are Nicodemus' main concerns?

   What does Nicodemus' response to Jesus reveal about his own spiritual life? (*Hint:* See John 3:2, 4, 9.)

3. How do you navigate situations that you find yourself in where the spiritual image you want to project is at odds with what's most true about you?

John hinted at this concept of rebirth or being born from above in the first chapter when he wrote, "But as many as received Him, to them He gave the right to become children of God, even to those who believe in His name, who were born, not of blood nor of the will of the flesh nor of the will of man, but of God" (John 1:12–13 NASB).

Yet this was not the only concept that was hard for Nicodemus to grasp. The idea that God loves the whole world must have been challenging as well. Jews rarely acknowledged God loving the world, only Israel. The idea that everyone is invited to believe and become a transformed child of God, empowered by the Spirit, through being born from above probably challenged Nicodemus on several levels.

> **Notable**
>
> Jesus' reference to Moses lifting up the snake in the desert (John 3:14–15) can be found in Numbers 21:4–9 and highlights the need for Christ's gift of salvation.

4. Why do you think the concept of being born from above is so hard for people to grasp even today? In your own words, how would you explain being born from above or born again to someone?

5. According to John 3, what happens to those who choose to believe in Jesus? (*Hint:* See vv. 16, 18, 36.)

6. Like Nicodemus, are there any areas or situations in your life where you struggle to believe God? What makes it especially difficult for you to trust God in this area of your life?

Spend some time prayerfully acknowledging any areas of your life where you struggle to believe God. Ask God to give you the faith to believe.

DAY FIVE: A Questionable Woman

John 4:1–41

Jesus turned water into wine at a wedding celebration, made a scene with moneychangers in the temple, and engaged in a nighttime theological conversation with a leading rabbi. Now John describes Jesus' encounter with a morally questionable woman at high noon at a well in Samaria. This is an unlikely meeting for multiple reasons, but John uses it to paint a beautiful portrait of redemption.

Strictly devout Jews avoided Samaria at all costs — especially when traveling from Jerusalem to Galilee — by taking the longer route around the region. Yet Jesus doesn't go around Samaria on his journey; he goes straight for it! The Scripture notes that Jesus "had to go" to Samaria (John 4:4), implying a divine leading to this region that was considered detestable by the Jews. Once he arrives, Jesus engages in a conversation with a woman who is viewed as detestable even by the Samaritans.

1. Read John 4:1–26. How does Jesus' introductory statement, "Give Me a drink" (John 4:7 NASB), set the scene for the conversation that follows?

Quotable

"When Jesus talks to her and begins to speak about personal things, such as her many ex-husbands, she changes the subject to something controversial: the differences in worship between her people and the Jews. The goal isn't to gain more knowledge as much as to throw the Rabbi off her trail. It's a smoke screen to change subjects once Jesus talks about her life."[3]

—Bill McCready

2. How does the woman respond when Jesus tells her she has had five husbands and the man she is living with is not her husband (John 4:17–18)?

How might you have responded if Jesus, a stranger, named your past and current sins?

3. Read John 4:27–38. What parallels do you see between the disciples' misunderstanding of food (4:31–33) and the woman's misunderstanding of water (4:15)?

How does Jesus leverage her misunderstandings to reveal more about himself and God?

Notable

The Samaritans acknowledge Jesus as the "Savior of the world" (John 4:42). The only other time this expression occurs in the New Testament is 1 John 4:14. The title suggests that Jesus is the one who delivers and saves from disaster. The reference to "world" suggests that Jesus didn't just come for one people group but for all people everywhere.

4. Read John 4:39–45. Why do you think the woman's fellow villagers listened to her when she returned from the well and told them about Jesus?

5. The Samaritan woman's story is a reminder that just because you may have a tarnished history in your community doesn't mean you can't share what God has done in your life. Sometimes the story will actually have

a bigger effect, not a lesser one. The Samaritan woman used her story (about Jesus knowing her as well as her failures and sins) to tell others about Christ. What is the one thing in your life for which you are most grateful for God's forgiveness and redemption?

6. Rather than hiding your past sins, your past failures — the things for which you have received God's forgiveness — there may be something you can share with others as a way of telling the story of what God has done for you. Who in your life might benefit from hearing your story?

Spend some time reflecting on the work God has done in your life. How can you be more intentional about reaching out and responding to God's presence in your life? Where are the modern-day wells in your community where you can go to engage people and share the love of Christ with them? Prayerfully consider how God may want you to engage others like the Samaritan woman.

When God Sees through You

John 4–8

> Never lose an opportunity of seeing anything that is beautiful; for beauty is God's handwriting — a wayside sacrament. Welcome it in every fair face, in every fair sky, in every fair flower, and thank God for it as a cup of blessing.
> —*Ralph Waldo Emerson*

The human heart is embedded with an unquenchable desire for beauty. The longing for beauty expresses itself in the details of everyday life — the use of a decorative tablecloth, a fresh bouquet of flowers, a silver button on a coat. The desire for beauty awakens something in us whether lingering to watch a canary-yellow ball of fire melt into the horizon on a summer's eve or waiting for that same heavenly object to glide into the sky during a late winter morning.

God instilled in us a desire for beauty so that we would long for God from whom all beauty emanates. Though we are created to find ourselves captivated by God, we often find ourselves distracted by the imperfections in our world and ourselves. When we look at the reflection of our own humanity, we can't help but shrink back at the frailty, the flaws, the defects, and the deficiencies. At times, we want to hide. Yet God continues pursuing us, exposing those areas so they can be restored and we can walk in the wholeness and beauty God intended all along. In the process, God performs a beautiful work in our lives.

Throughout the Gospel of John, Jesus reveals that which is hidden, those areas which hold people back from believing in him. Jesus doesn't just see people; he sees through them. The Son of God sees through their facades and efforts to make a good first impression, straight to their hearts. John describes Jesus as a light that penetrates the darkness, revealing things we may not want to be seen. Often such exposure is the first step toward believing and experiencing God's healing and redemption.

Getting Started: Select One

Experiential Activity: Hidden Pictures

What you'll need:

◆ Images that contain hidden pictures

◆ Photocopies of the images or a laptop and video projector to display the images

1. Selected a handful of images that contain hidden pictures from books like the Where's Waldo? series or a *Highlights* magazine. Google the work of Liu Bolin, a camouflage master who creates unusual artwork.
2. Distribute photocopies* to participants or display the pictures on a laptop or projector and spend about 5 minutes hunting for the hidden images.
3. Discuss the following questions:

   • What does it feel like to find a hidden image?

   • Once you recognize the hidden image, is it hard for you *not* to see it? Why or why not?

---

*Be sure to note if there are any restrictions on duplicating the image or if it is necessary to secure permission to reproduce the image.

Icebreaker Question

If you're not doing the experiential activity, choose one *of the following sets of questions to begin your discussion.*

   • What advice would you suggest for newcomers to your area to get to know people?

   • When you feel threatened, do you tend to go into fight mode, flight mode, or freeze mode? Why do you think you choose that mode of response?

   • The Bible never tells us the name of the woman whom Jesus met at the well, but imagine that you had the opportunity to meet her and give her a name. What name would you give her that represents her life *before* meeting Jesus and *after* meeting Jesus?

Two: When God Sees through You

As you watch the DVD, use the following outline to take notes on anything that stands out to you.

I sometimes convince myself that somehow God doesn't see me. That somehow I, too, can hide in plain sight.

Jesus knows that defilement or real dirtiness doesn't come from the outside but the inside — that our worst enemy is not "those people" but ourselves.

"Give me a drink." With only four words, Jesus breaks down the barriers of gender, politics, and religion.

The Samaritan woman cannot contain the good news. She becomes the first recognized female evangelist.

Though we try to empty our bag of tricks — standing perfectly still, moving excessively fast, or diverting attention elsewhere — God sees and exposes us. The exposure is always an invitation to healing, restoration, and wholeness.

(30–45 MINUTES)

1. Consider what you learned about this beautiful portrait of redemption in the life of the Samaritan woman from the Afterhours personal studies or on the DVD. What caught your attention or stood out most to you?

Reaching Out to "Those People"

2. Take turns reading John 4:1–42. The passage makes it clear that Jews in Jesus' day held many prejudices about Samaritans. Who would you say are the Samaritans in our society? Identify eight to ten types of people who might be classified as social outcasts — those who are marginalized or considered misfits — or those in our society whom religious people especially might look down on.

What characteristics do these groups share?

Notable

Calling a Jewish person a Samaritan was considered a hostile insult in ancient culture.

3. Have you ever been the one who is marginalized or looked down on? How did you handle the situation?

4. How do you tend to respond to people who are different from you?

5. What makes it difficult for you to relate to or reach out to the Samaritans in your own life?

Overcoming the Force Field

One of the ways Jesus demonstrates love for the Samaritan woman is by not excusing or overlooking what she's done (John 4:16–18). Jesus doesn't just see the Samaritan woman; he sees through her actions and responses and identifies the deeper issues in her life.

6. What does it mean to have compassion on those who are struggling with sin without overlooking or approving the sin? When have you experienced such a response from others in your own spiritual journey?

> **Quotable**
>
> "A feature of this story is the way the woman persistently attempts to avoid the issues that Jesus raises. But just as persistently Jesus brings her back to them until finally he secures the desired result."[4]
>
> —Leon Morris

7. After encountering Jesus, the woman left her water jar at the well. Why do you think the woman left her jar?

What do you think the water jar symbolizes or represents in the life of the Samaritan woman (John 4:28)?

Exposed to God's Healing

8. Pair up with one other person. Take turns reading aloud each of the passages listed on the chart that follows. After each passage, briefly discuss what the passage reveals about God's mercy and compassion and how you see these same truths reflected in the story of Jesus and the Samaritan woman. Briefly note your responses in the space provided.

Scripture	God's mercy and compassion in Scripture	Jesus' mercy and compassion for the Samaritan woman
Exodus 33:19	*Example: God has mercy and compassion on those he wishes.*	*Example: Jesus shows mercy and compassion toward the Samaritan woman.*
Deuteronomy 4:30–31		
Psalm 103:13		
Hebrews 4:15–16		

9. Read Revelation 7:16–17. What hope is promised for those who thirst and hunger?

In what ways would this passage be a source of comfort for both the Samaritan woman and the disciples?

In what ways does this passage comfort you?

10. While knowing that God sees everything can be challenging and make us wish that we could leave some things in the dark, there's also great comfort in this truth. What comfort do you find in knowing that God sees everything in your life? What are you glad that God sees and knows?

 Close in Prayer

Ask God to:

- Reveal areas in your life that need healing, restoration, and wholeness.
- Trade any ashes in your life for beauty.
- Help you find opportunities to reach out to those on the margins of your community and share God's love and faithfulness.

Jumpstart

To get an insider's look at the Pursuing God series, bonus features, and freebies, as well as join the online discussion, visit *www.pursuinggodbiblestudy.com*.

To prepare for the next group session, read John 9 and tackle the Afterhours personal studies.

Afterhours Personal Studies

Dive deeper into John's Gospel by engaging in these five personal studies. If you only have time for one, choose Day Five, which will prepare you specifically for the next session.

DAY ONE: Divine Healings and Declarations
John 4:46–John 5:45

After spending time in Samaria, Jesus returns to Cana where he performed the miracle of making water into wine and performs another miracle (John 4:54). This particular miracle is unusual in that it's one of the long-distance miracles that Jesus performed (see Matthew 8:5–13; Luke 7:1–19). The act highlights Jesus' divinity as well as the royal official's faith.

1. Read John 4:46–54. What do you find surprising in the royal official's response to Jesus (vv. 48–49)?

   Would you have responded to Jesus in the same way after hearing his comment? Why or why not?

After returning to Cana, Jesus travels back to Jerusalem for an unspecified feast. Walking by the pool at Bethesda, Jesus has compassion on a specific man who had been sick for 38 years. In a strikingly beautiful moment, Jesus heals him.

> **Notable**
>
> Some scholars believe the "sheep gate" (Nehemiah 3:1, 32; 12:39) was a small opening in the temple wall where the sheep entered and were washed before being taken into the sanctuary for sacrifice. The nearby pool became a waiting area for the sick and disabled who hoped for a miraculous healing.

2. Read John 5:1–17. Why do you think the response to the healing of the official's son is so much different than the response to the healing of the sick man at the pool of Bethesda?

   What three things does Jesus do and say that make the Jews so angry? (*Hint:* See John 5:9, 16–18.)

3. The story focuses more on the controversy that follows the healing rather than the healing itself. Why is this significant?

   Do you tend to become more or less involved in religious communities that are concerned with controversy? Explain.

Opposition toward Jesus grows to the point the Jews want to kill Jesus. Jesus offers a response in the form of a monologue. The lack of follow-up questions from listeners may suggest that Jesus silenced their concerns (though opposition only increases in upcoming chapters) or may suggest a literary device used in John's Gospel to sum up Jesus' thoughts on a situation.

4. Read John 5:18–47. What are the primary claims Jesus makes within this passage?

Scripture	Jesus' claim	Why this claim would anger the Jewish religious leaders
John 5:18	*Example: God as his Father; making himself equal with God*	*Example: The Jews thought it was wrong to claim to be equal with God.*
John 5:24		
John 5:27, 30		
John 5:46–47		

5. In this monologue, Jesus names four witnesses that affirm his identity as the Messiah. Who/what are they? (*Hint:* See John 5:33, 36, 37, 39.)

Where do you turn when you need your faith strengthened?

6. The first five chapters of John offer beautiful stories of Jesus' miracles and teachings. Through Jesus, God's life-giving activity is unleashed among the people. Jesus' teachings confirm what people are seeing and experiencing through the miracles. Which of the miracles Jesus performed is most meaningful to you in your own faith journey right now?

Spend some time reflecting on the claims Jesus makes in John 5 about who he really is. Prayerfully ask God to make these claims more real in your own life. Over the upcoming week, keep an eye out for people and situations that witness that Jesus is the Messiah.

DAY TWO: Unforgettable Miracles Surrounding the Passover
John 6

Jesus displays the beauty and wonder of his divinity through a wide array of miracles and rich teachings in the first five chapters of John's Gospel. In the sixth chapter, Passover is mentioned for a second time. This is significant to the events that are about to unfold. During the Passover, the Jewish people studied the Scriptures that described the Israelites' escape from Egypt. They were reading about God's miraculous provision and protection—the narrow escape through the Red Sea and the feeding of the Israelites in the desert—when Jesus performs two unforgettable miracles.

Jesus is attracting sizeable crowds. Some want to hear his teachings, but many just want to see the healings and miracles. Looking out on the thousands of followers, many of whom have traveled long distances, Jesus performs a miracle that is reminiscent of God feeding the Israelites in the desert.

1. Read John 6:1–14. Jesus already knows he is going to perform a miracle. Jesus asks Philip where to buy bread, but Philip is too distracted by the cost of feeding so many people. Meanwhile, Andrew finds the only source of bread and fish available, but then questions how the food could ever be enough. Philip becomes overwhelmed by the size of the issue; Andrew becomes overwhelmed by the insufficiency of a possible solution. Neither recognizes Jesus' ability to perform the miraculous. When you are faced with a difficult challenge, does your response tend to be more like Philip's or Andrew's? Why?

2. Read John 6:14–25. Jesus identifies himself to the disciples as "It is I" when approaching them on the water (John 6:20). Throughout the Gospel of John, Jesus proclaims multiple "I AM" statements. The Greek *ego eimi* is emphatic—literally translating "I, I am." The words are reminiscent of God revealing himself as "I AM" in Exodus 3:14. If Jesus' feeding of the multitude is reminiscent of God providing for the Israelites in the desert (Exodus 16), then what is Jesus' walking on the water reminiscent of in the history of the Israelites? (*Hint:* See Exodus 13–15.)

Jesus knows the response of the people to the miracle will be to take him by force and make him king. Jesus withdraws to the mountains near Galilee. The disciples travel ahead by boat to Capernaum.

The miracles of feeding the five thousand and walking on water demonstrate that Jesus is the Messiah and fulfilling the role of God. Jesus is feeding, providing, protecting, guarding, rescuing, leading, and teaching. Though the people face challenges on every front—from lack of food to severe weather—Jesus overcomes every one. The miracles Jesus performs are reminiscent of God's care for the Israelites surrounding the events of Passover.

3. Read John 6:26–40. What does Jesus communicate about the true bread of God in the following verses?

Scripture	True bread of God
John 6:32	*Example: The bread that was provided in the desert didn't come from Moses, but from God.*
John 6:33	
John 6:34	

4. Read John 6:41–65. What portion of this teaching do you think was the hardest for the Jews to believe? Why?

What portion of this teaching is the hardest for you to believe?

Bonus Activity

The Israelites were known as God's chosen people in the Old Testament. Jesus now refers to his disciples, the community of believers, as those he has chosen (John 6:70). Read Numbers 11. What parallels do you see between the miracle of Jesus providing for the multitudes and God providing for the Israelites?

---

5. Read John 6:66–71. How does the response of many of the disciples (v. 66) compare with Peter's response (vv. 68–69)?

What does this passage reveal about what it means to believe in Jesus?

6. In what areas of your own spiritual life do you find yourself struggling with unbelief?

Spend some time prayerfully reflecting on John 6 and the teachings of Jesus. Ask God to reveal any areas of unbelief in your life. Ask God for the wisdom, grace, and courage to believe. Ask God to give you a spiritual appetite for the food which endures.

Opposition and controversy surround Jesus on every side. Even his own family members are questioning his identity. Though they've seen the miracles, they refuse to believe. John's Gospel is written so that people might believe in Jesus, but this chapter reveals that many people choose to oppose Jesus instead.

1. Read John 7:1–53. What criticism, hostility, or opposition does Jesus face in each of the following passages? On a scale of 1 to 10, how would you rate the level of criticism, hostility, or opposition?

Scripture	Criticism, hostility, or opposition faced	Level of opposition
John 7:1	*Example: Jews are trying to kill Jesus.*	*Example: 10*
John 7:5		
John 7:7		
John 7:12		
John 7:15		
John 7:20		
John 7:27		
John 7:30		
John 7:32		
John 7:42		
John 7:43		

Among the examples of criticism, hostility, and opposition you listed on the chart, which two or three do you think are most often expressed about Jesus today?

2. How does Jesus respond to the criticism, hostility, and opposition he faces?

What insights do you gain from Jesus' example about how to face criticism, hostility, or opposition in your own life?

> **Notable**
>
> Jesus is questioned on where he went to school (John 7:15), where he is from (John 7:27), and where he is going (John 7:35). The irony is, the answer to all three questions is the same: heaven.

Jews in Jesus' day traveled to Jerusalem for three annual feasts — the Feast of Passover (mentioned three times in John's Gospel), the Feast of Pentecost which is seven weeks after the Passover and celebrates the harvest of grain, and the Feast of Tabernacles which celebrates the fall harvest. Jesus often uses images from these festivals in his teachings. In the seventh chapter of John, Jesus draws on rich imagery from the Feast of Tabernacles.

The Feast of Tabernacles is also referred to as the Feast of Booths or Ingathering because, in order to protect the harvest, farmers had to build shelters in the fields. The image of a temporary shelter is reminiscent of the temporary shelters the Israelites built in the desert to survive. Thus, the Feast of Tabernacles, or Sukkot, which is still celebrated today, is more than a fall harvest; the holy days are used to study and reflect on the desert wanderings of the Israelites.

Sacrifices were offered throughout the seven-day Festival of the Tabernacles celebration. Since fall is a dry season, requests were also made for rain, including a water ceremony in which a priest filled a golden pitcher with water as a choir quoted Isaiah 12:3. The water was then carried back up to the "Water Gate" at the temple with crowds singing Psalms 113–118. Then the water was poured out on the altar as an offering. On the final day of the Feast of Tabernacles, the water ceremony was repeated seven times.[5]

3. Reflecting on the context of this scene, why are Jesus' statements in John 7:37–39 significant?

4. How do you respond to opposition and criticism in your life?

5. On the continuum below, how would you rate your own response to opposition and criticism?

A HEALTHY RESPONSE   UNHEALTHY RESPONSE

6. What steps can you take to developing or maintaining a healthy response to criticism and opposition?

Ask God to give you wisdom and grace to face opposition and criticism. Then spend some time asking God to unleash rivers of living water in your life. Ask God to both increase and quench your spiritual thirst.

DAY FOUR: A Spiritual Ambush

John 8

Jesus travels to the Mount of Olives. As if Jesus isn't surrounded by enough controversy, he's now faced with a spiritual ambush. The religious leaders present Jesus with a woman caught in adultery, but her story is only incidental to the main show—forcing Jesus to make a judgment on a hot-button issue.

1. Read John 8:1 – 11. How would you describe the demeanor or attitude of the various people in the story?

The woman caught in adultery ...

The religious leaders ...

The onlookers ...

Jesus ...

Bonus Activity

For Old Testament background of the charges against the adulterous woman, read Leviticus 20:10 and Deuteronomy 22:22.

2. Some scholars suggest Jesus may have written Exodus 23:1 and Jeremiah 17:13 in the dust. Look up each passage. Why do you think scholars suggest these passages as the ones Jesus wrote in the dust?

After the woman accused of adultery goes free, Jesus makes some startling claims. Jesus declares himself the light of the world — a metaphor first introduced in John 1:4 – 5 — and then goes on to make even more provocative claims.

3. Read John 8:12 – 29. How do the Pharisees respond to Jesus' claim to be the light of the world (v. 13)?

How does Jesus answer the Pharisees (vv. 14 – 18)?

Why do you think Jesus' claim is so hard for the Pharisees to accept?

4. What controversial claim does Jesus make in each of the following verses?

Scripture	Controversial claim
John 8:19	*Example: He claims to be God's Son.*
John 8:24	
John 8:32	
John 8:42	
John 8:44	
John 8:58	

With each statement, tensions escalate between the religious leaders and Jesus. Every statement is met with misunderstanding and disbelief. The religious leaders accuse Jesus of being a Samaritan as well as being possessed by a demon. By claiming Jesus is a Samaritan, the religious leaders are severing him from any connection with Judaism and the children of Abraham. By claiming he has a demon, the religious leaders are trying to connect Jesus with the devil instead of God.

Despite the misunderstandings, attacks, and disbelief, Jesus continues to proclaim the good news and invite belief; whoever obeys his word, he says, will be spared and never taste death (John 8:51). This, too, is misunderstood and dismissed by the religious leaders (vv. 52–53).

The irony of this chapter is that it began with Jesus defending a woman from being stoned. Fifty-nine verses later the religious leaders are picking up rocks to stone Jesus.

5. Briefly review your responses to question 1. Throughout the course of your spiritual journey, in what ways, if any, have you responded to Jesus as those people did?

The woman caught in adultery ...

The religious leaders ...

The onlookers ...

Spend time in prayer asking God for what you need right now. Your requests may include humility, grace, peace, love, or greater compassion for others. Express your gratitude to God for the ways he has extended compassion to you.

DAY FIVE: Open the Eyes of Our Hearts

John 9

The healing of the blind man in John's Gospel is the sixth of John's seven signs. Here's a quick summary of all seven signs:

1. Changing water into wine (John 2:1 – 11).
2. Cleansing the temple (John 2:13 – 22).
3. Healing the nobleman's son (John 4:46 – 54).
4. Healing the lame man (John 5:1 – 15).
5. Feeding the multitude (John 6:1 – 15).
6. Healing the blind man (John 9:1 – 12).
7. Raising Lazarus from the dead (John 11). (We'll study this sign in session three.)

While healing the blind man is the sixth sign, it is only the third healing recorded in John's Gospel.

One can only imagine what the man's response was to all the beauty he encountered once his eyes were opened. Colors unimaginable. Hues unexpected. Inconceivable scenes surrounded him in every direction.

1. Read John 9:1 – 12. Restoring sight to the blind was known as a messianic sign in the Old Testament. Reflecting on the following passages, how does Jesus' healing recorded here in John reveal himself as the long-awaited and promised Messiah?

   Isaiah 29:18:

   Isaiah 35:5:

   Isaiah 42:7:

2. God can open physical eyes and God can open spiritual eyes, which are sometimes called the eyes of the heart. What would you like God to reveal to you or help you see more clearly in your life?

Jewish rabbis maintained a belief that suffering and sin were connected. Thus, the Jewish culture embraced the belief that any suffering was somehow linked to sin, whether or not it could be identified. While Jesus acknowledges that suffering can be a result of sin, it is not always the case and this truth will be demonstrated in the life of the blind man.

The healing of the blind man draws on two images that are used repeatedly in John's Gospel: water and light. Jesus reveals himself as the "living water" (John 7:38) and the "light of the world" (John 9:5).

Water references saturate the pages of John's Gospel:

- The book begins with John the Baptist baptizing people in the Jordan River (John 1:26).
- Jesus' first miracle is turning water into wine (John 2:6 – 9).

- Jesus tells Nicodemus of the importance of being born of water and spirit (John 3:5).
- Jesus meets the Samaritan woman at a well (John 4).
- Jesus displays his power by walking on water in the middle of a storm (John 6:16–19).
- When Jesus reveals himself as the "living water" he does so with the backdrop of the water ceremony as part of the Feast of Tabernacles (John 7:38).

Now Jesus places a blend of saliva and dirt on a blind man's eyes and sends him to wash in the Pool of Siloam, the very source of the water for the water-pouring ceremony at the Feast of Tabernacles.

References to light illuminate John's Gospel:

- Jesus is referred to as the light in the cosmic poem that opens the book (John 1:4–5, 9).
- Jesus reveals to Nicodemus that those who live by the truth enter the light (John 3:21).
- With the rich backdrop of the lighting ceremonies of the Feast of Tabernacles, Jesus reveals himself as the light of the world (John 8:12).
- Before opening the eyes of the blind man, Jesus announces that he's the light of the world (John 9:5).

The imagery of both water and light come together in the healing of the blind man, whose physical blindness is contrasted against the spiritual blindness of the religious leaders.

> **Notable**
>
> The opening of blind eyes is rare in the Old Testament (2 Kings 6:8–23) and described under unusual circumstances. Jesus' healing of a man who was born blind is extraordinary.

3. In what ways is the beautiful healing of the blind man a fulfillment of Jesus' claim to be the light of the world?

4. Read John 9:13–41. Why do you think the healing of the blind man creates such a controversy?

How do you think the blind man felt as he experienced healing?

How do you think the blind man felt when he heard the reaction from the following people?

Neighbors . . .

Religious leaders . . .

His own parents . . .

Which do you think was the most hurtful? Why?

5. The Pharisees excommunicate the blind man, but Jesus seeks him out — another example of how Jesus takes the initiative to pursue those he loves. We saw this in session one when Jesus sought out his disciples, calling them to follow him (page 15). In what ways do you think Jesus may be pursuing you right now — to bring something hidden to light, to give your thirsty soul a drink of cold water, or to help you in some other way?

Spend time prayerfully asking God to reveal himself as the light of your life and to unleash his light in the deepest areas of your being. Ask God to create opportunities for you to shine his light to the world.

Recognizing the Blind Spots

John 9–11

In a gracious gratitude men are affected with the attribute of God's goodness and free grace not only as they are concerned in it, or as it affects their interest, but as part of the glory and beauty of God's nature. That wonderful and unparalleled grace of God, which is manifested in the work of redemption, and shines forth in the face of Jesus Christ, is infinitely glorious in itself and appears so to the angels; it is a great part of the moral perfection and beauty of God's nature.[6]

—*Jonathan Edwards*

Though the beauty of God beckons us, we can close our eyes to God's beauty—not only in creation but in our own lives. We can become blind to the moments when God wants to apprehend us with goodness, call us to holiness, and ignite our hearts with love.

All of us have blurred vision in one area or another. We also have blind spots—both physically and spiritually. Yet Jesus is the one who opens our eyes so that we can see clearly and recognize the beautiful work he's doing in our lives. May we live with eyes wide open to recognize the beauty of God in all its expressions.

Getting Started: Select One

Experiential Activity: The Role of Sight

What you'll need:

- ◆ Three to five simple and tasty foods for people to eat
- ◆ A few blindfolds—bandanas or scarves work well

1. Purchase three to five different yummy foods that require little to no preparation to eat (for example, apples, honeydew, cupcakes, crackers, and cheese).
2. Ask participants to close their eyes and tie on a blindfold.
3. Distribute food samples one at a time.*
4. Invite participants to taste the food and to identify it with as much precision as possible. For example, if they're eating a bite of apple, can they identify the type of apple—Honeycrisp, Granny Smith, or Fuji? If they are eating a cupcake, can they identify the flavor?
5. Spend some time enjoying the leftover snacks and discuss these questions:

   - What role does sight play in enjoying food?
   - What would you miss the most if you were unable to see?
   - What would you miss the least?

   *Check to see if anyone has food allergies before serving samples.

Icebreaker Question

If you're not doing the experiential activity, choose one *of the following sets of questions to begin your discussion.*

- Do you or any of your friends have an issue with your vision that inhibits your everyday life? What do you think are the biggest challenges of vision impairment? Are there any upsides to not being able to see as well?
- If you had to lose one of your senses (taste, touch, smell, hearing, or sight), which would you live without? Why did you choose it?
- Share a childhood memory in which you were confronted or surrounded by darkness. What did you feel and experience at that moment? How did the experience shape you?

Three: Recognizing the Blind Spots

As you watch the DVD, use the following outline to take notes on anything that stands out to you.

What's wrong with my driving?

We all see things differently. We notice different details. And we all have blind spots — both physically and spiritually.

Instead of responding with celebration and joy to this beautiful moment, they begin interrogating the blind man.

The whole story raises the question of how often God wants to expose a blind spot in my life, and I respond like the religious leaders.

Something about being confronted by the miraculous, the transformative power of God, exposes the blind spots in our lives.

Sometimes we forget that even if we score perfectly on Bible tests, it doesn't mean our vision is 20/20.

👥 Group Discussion Questions

1. Consider what you learned about this beautiful portrait of healing in the life of the blind man from the Afterhours personal studies or on the DVD. What caught your attention or stood out most to you?

Blind from Birth

2. Read John 9:1 – 12. Jesus said, "I am the light of the world." How have you experienced Jesus as a light in your own life? In other words, how has Christ's life and teaching helped you to see things — spiritual truth, personal failures, goodness — you might otherwise have missed?

How has your life been transformed by this beautiful light?

Notable

Jesus heals a deaf and mute man in Mark 7 by applying saliva to the man's tongue and again in Mark 8 when he touches a blind man's eyes with saliva. Saliva was believed to have medicinal healing ability in the ancient world. Some even believed it had magical powers, which led to its use for healing being forbidden in the Jewish community.

3. After rubbing mud on the man's eyes, Jesus tells the man born blind to go and wash in the pool of Siloam. Why do you think Jesus makes such a specific yet odd demand?

4. Why do you think Jesus sometimes instantaneously heals people but at other times requires that the person make an additional effort? (See Mark 3:1–6; John 5:1–15.)

How have you experienced spiritual growth and healing in your own life? Has it been instantaneous, a step-by-step process, or perhaps a mix? Share examples, if possible, to illustrate your response.

The Controversy Brews

5. The healing of the blind man creates quite a controversy. What is the response of each of the following individuals or groups of people to the healing?

The neighbors (John 9:8–10) ...

The Pharisees (John 9:15–17) ...

The Jews (John 9:18) ...

The parents (John 9:20–23) ...

6. Despite the healing of the blind man, many still refuse to believe that Jesus is the Messiah. Are there spiritual truths you resist — things you know are true but struggle to receive or act on? What keeps you from accepting some spiritual truths?

> ### Notable
>
> Blind Spot (noun): 1. a small area on the retina that is insensitive to light due to the interruption, where the optic nerve joins the retina, of the normal pattern of light-sensitive rods and cones. 2. An area or subject about which one is uninformed, prejudiced, or unappreciative.[7]

7. The religious leaders are so caught up in rules and regulations that they miss the bigger picture and the miraculous evidence of God's grace among them. Do you think this dynamic — focusing on rules to the point of missing grace — is a problem in the Christian community today? Why or why not?

In what ways, if any, have you experienced this dynamic — either as the person caught up in focusing on the rules or as the recipient of graceless scrutiny from others?

8. Read John 9:35–41. Why do you think Jesus seeks out the man a second time? What does this reveal about the character of Jesus?

Reflecting on the Afterhours study (session two, Day Five, pages 53–56), how is this consistent with the message of John's Gospel?

Only Jesus Sees Clearly

9. How would you describe what it means to have a blind spot? If you can think of any, illustrate your response with an example from your own experience or from that of someone you know (without revealing the person's name).

If you had a blind spot about something in your life, how would you want someone to tell you about it? What could this person say or do to help you be more receptive to feedback that might be hard for you to hear?

Quotable

"Christ is the genuine light. He is the light that brings real illumination to men. There is nothing unreal or shadowy about the light which is Christ."[8]

—Leon Morris

---

10. Jesus healed the man born blind to demonstrate the glory of God. What areas of your life — those marked by illness, weakness, failure, or inability — might God use to demonstrate his glory and beauty in your life?

Like the blind man in John's Gospel, we all have areas of our lives that we don't see clearly. Our vision is distorted and blurred and we need Jesus to open our eyes and restore our vision so we can clearly see the beautiful work that God wants to do not only in our lives but also in the lives of those around us.

Close in Prayer

Ask God to:

- Reveal any blind spots.
- Give you his vision by helping you to see yourself and others through God's eyes.
- Help you to see people or situations where you might share God's love, beauty, and goodness.

 ## Jumpstart

To get an insider's look at the Pursuing God series, bonus features, and freebies, as well as join the online discussion, visit *www.pursuinggodbiblestudy.com.*

To prepare for the next group session, read John 12:1 – 11 and tackle the Afterhours personal studies.

Afterhours Personal Studies

Dive deeper into John's Gospel by engaging in these five personal studies. If you only have time for one, choose Day Five, which will prepare you specifically for the next session.

DAY ONE: **The Beautiful Shepherd**

John 10:1–21

Following the healing of the blind man, the Pharisees find themselves struggling to swallow Jesus' teaching. Jesus couldn't possibly be saying they're blind, could he?

Jesus affirms that because they refuse to acknowledge their blindness, because they refuse the light and the message of Jesus, they remain in the darkness of their sin. Jesus uses shepherding imagery in order to expose the hardness of their hearts and reveal himself again as the Messiah. In the process, he exposes the beautiful heart of God for each of us.

The Greek word *kalos*, which translates "good" as in "good shepherd," can also be translated as "excellent" or "beautiful." In describing himself as the good shepherd, Jesus reveals himself as the "beautiful shepherd." The beauty is displayed both in his heart and passion for the sheep as well as in his willingness to sacrifice his own life for the sheep.

1. Read John 10:1 – 21. Jesus' teaching describes three different types of groups caring for sheep: thieves, hirelings, true shepherds. According to this passage, how would you describe the characteristics of each group?

   Thieves . . .

   Hirelings . . .

True shepherds ...

The imagery of thieves and hirelings (as opposed to true shepherds) is an indictment against the leaders of Israel who do not really love God and God's people. The imagery is used throughout the Old Testament in passages such as Psalm 23, Psalm 95, and Isaiah 40:11.

2. Read Ezekiel 34. What parallels do you see between the prophet's words to the religious leaders of Israel and Jesus' words to the religious leaders of Israel? Reflecting on the descriptions in this passage, in what ways have you felt led by the following?

Thieves ...

Hirelings ...

Good shepherds ...

Bonus Activity

To better understand sheep and shepherds as well as to expose some of the modern myths about sheep (i.e., the idea that they are dumb), consider reading my book *Scouting the Divine: My Search for God in Wine, Wool, and Wild Honey*.

3. What do Ezekiel 34 and John 10:1–21 reveal about God's love for you?

4. What do you believe Jesus means when he says that his sheep listen to the shepherd's voice (John 10:4)?

How do you hear and recognize God's voice in your own life?

Jesus' teaching is again met with division and a refusal to believe. Those listening accuse Jesus of having a demon and being out of his right mind just as they did in John 8:48–52. Other listeners are still debating whether Jesus really healed the blind man in John 9:16, 32–33.

> **Notable**
>
> Before becoming a king, David was a shepherd. He is known for risking his own life for his flock in 1 Samuel 17:34–37.

5. In light of Jesus' teaching on beautiful and good shepherding, what do the religious leaders' responses reveal about their relationship to the Beautiful and Good Shepherd?

What does Jesus' teaching reveal about how they have cared for the flock, the people of God?

6. In what ways do you need Jesus to be your good shepherd right now?

Spend some time in prayer, inviting Christ to be the Good and Beautiful Shepherd who guides and protects you. You may want to use Psalm 23 as the basis for your prayer and to express gratitude for the ways God leads, guides, restores, and anoints as he shepherds you.

John 10:22–42

The eight-day Feast of Dedication, also known as Hanukkah or the Feast of Lights, finds its origins in a historic event. In 167 BC, Antiochus Epiphanes captured Jerusalem and committed all kinds of atrocious acts, including erecting an altar to Zeus and offering sacrifices to Zeus in the Jewish temple. The sacrilegious acts incited guerilla warfare and, three years later, under the leadership of Judas (the Maccabee), Jerusalem was freed.

Legend has it that when the Jewish priests reentered the temple for the first time, they found a portion of holy oil sufficient to fuel a menorah (a candelabrum with nine branches) for a single day. Instead, it burned for eight days. This is the miracle celebrated today as Hanukkah, a word derived from the Hebrew verb meaning "to dedicate." During the Festival of Dedication, Jewish families use brightly lit candles and lamps throughout their homes as part of their holiday celebration.

1. Read John 10:22–42. Throughout John's Gospel, feasts and festivals are commonly used as a backdrop to the teachings of Jesus. Why might John mention the Feast of Dedication to set the stage for this particular interaction between Jesus and the religious leaders?

2. Up until this moment in John's Gospel, Jesus has only revealed himself directly as the Messiah to the Samaritan woman (John 4:26), yet he's demonstrated the fact through signs, miracles, and teachings. Why do you think the Jews are still asking Jesus to tell them plainly if he's the Messiah?

Notable

John 10:22 notes a somewhat odd detail, namely, that it was winter. While some scholars argue that this detail explained why Jesus was in the sheltered area of the portico of Solomon, some suggest the wintry mention is representative of the cold attitude toward Jesus and the icy receptivity of his listeners.

---

3. Reflecting on the previous sessions and the Afterhours studies thus far, do you think Jesus has made it clear enough to the people that he is the Messiah? Why or why not?

4. Do you feel any frustration toward the people's unbelief? Why or why not? How do you think your feelings compare to what Jesus felt?

5. Read Leviticus 24:14. Do you think the Jews' response to Jesus in John 10:31 is appropriate based on this passage? How does Jesus answer the Jews? (*Hint:* See Psalm 82:6).

6. What comfort do you find in Jesus' promise that no one shall snatch from his hand those he gives eternal life (John 10:28)?

Spend time prayerfully reflecting on the promise that no one can snatch you out of Jesus' hand. Take a few moments to thank God for the faithfulness, love, and goodness that he's shown you.

DAY THREE: The Resurrection Power of Jesus
John 11

With opposition mounting against Jesus, he withdraws to the Jordan where John the Baptist was first baptizing. As many people come to him there and believe his message, Jesus receives word from one of his supporters and followers, Mary, that her brother Lazarus is extremely ill. Rather than drop what he's doing, Jesus offers a surprising response that is reminiscent of his words about the man born blind. The sickness won't lead to death but to God's glory.

1. Read John 11:1 – 16. How do you resolve the conflict between Jesus' love and care for Lazarus and his deliberate choice to delay responding to Lazarus' illness?

When Jesus tells the disciples that Lazarus has fallen asleep, the disciples misinterpret Jesus and take his statement literally. Similar misinterpretations happened with the woman at the well (liquid water versus living water) and Nicodemus (physical birth versus spiritual birth). Jesus plainly tells the disciples that Lazarus is dead.

2. Read John 11:17 – 37. Each time Jesus is misunderstood in John's Gospel, it creates an opportunity for Jesus to reveal more about God, himself, and what he's about to do. How does Martha misunderstand what Jesus is saying (John 11:23 – 27)?

Notable

The name Lazarus means "whom God helps."

3. How does Jesus respond to Mary, Martha, and the others who are mourning (John 11:33 – 35)?

Does anything surprise you or comfort you about Jesus' response?

4. Read John 11:38 – 46. What does this beautiful miracle reveal about Jesus' identity and mission?

5. Read John 11:47–54. What are the two different responses—the chief priests and Pharisees versus Caiaphas—toward Jesus in this passage?

What do these responses reveal about God's work in the listeners' lives?

6. In what area of your life do you most need to experience the resurrecting power of Jesus?

Spend some time asking God to reveal his resurrection power to you. Ask God to do the impossible in a specific area of your life.

DAY FOUR: The Great "I Am" Statements

Throughout John's Gospel, Jesus makes a series of "I am" sayings. The use of the "I am" is reminiscent of the name God used to reveal himself to Moses during his encounter at the burning bush in Exodus 3.

Just as the seven signs in John's Gospel reveal Jesus as the Messiah, seven "I am" statements reveal Jesus' identity, not only as the way to God but also as God. Each "I am" statement reflects a motif from Judaism that challenges listeners to recognize who Jesus is and believe in him.

1. Look up each of the following passages and record the "I am" statements in the space below:

Scripture	"I am" statement
John 6:35	
John 8:12	

(cont.)

Scripture	"I am" statement
John 10:7	
John 10:11	
John 11:25	
John 14:6	
John 15:1	

2. Jesus claims to be the bread of life (John 6:35), the spiritual food we need. Read Exodus 16:13 – 18. How does God reveal himself as the bread of life in this passage?

   What similarities and differences do you recognize between the two kinds of spiritual sustenance — manna and Christ?

   What spiritual nourishment are you most hungry for right now?

3. Jesus claims to be the light of the world (John 8:12). Read Genesis 1:3, Psalm 27:1, and Psalm 36:9. How does God reveal himself as the light of the world in these passages?

   What areas of your life do you most need the light of God to shine in?

4. Jesus reveals himself as the gate of the sheep pen and the good shepherd (John 10:7, 11). Read Psalm 23 and Ezekiel 34. How does God reveal himself as the keeper of the sheep in these passages?

How is God revealing himself as the good shepherd in your life right now?

5. Jesus describes himself as the resurrection, the way, the truth, and the life (John 11:25, 14:6). Read Deuteronomy 32:39, Psalm 86:11, and Proverbs 15:24. How does God reveal himself in similar terms in these passages?

How have you experienced God as the resurrection, the way, the truth, and the life? Are there any areas in which you have yet to experience him in these ways?

6. Jesus describes God as the vine keeper (John 15:1). Read Psalm 80:8–19 and Jeremiah 2:21–22. How does God reveal himself as the vintner or vine keeper in these passages?

Which of the metaphors or images from this personal study are most meaningful to you in your personal walk with God right now? Why?

Spend some time asking God to reveal himself more deeply and personally to you in each of these beautiful ways.

DAY FIVE: A Beautiful Act of Worship

John 12:1–11

While hosting Jesus, the disciples, and various guests, Mary does something extraordinary. Mary's beautiful act probably silences the room as people watch in a strange mix of awe, wonder, and contempt.

1. Read John 12:1–11. If you were watching Mary, what might you have found most disturbing about her actions?

What would you have found to be most beautiful about her actions?

Notable

The Greek word for "poured" also means "anoint." The anointing of a king by pouring oil on his head at coronation was observed not only in Israel but in other countries (Judges 9:8, 15; 1 Samuel 9:16).

2. Read John 1:27 and John 13:5. Attending to someone's feet was the work of servants. What does Mary's action reveal about her attitude toward and relationship with Christ?

3. While it's impossible to know what compelled Mary to pour out a pint of pure nard, Jesus gives the worshipful expression a theological meaning, saying the oil was poured out for his burial. (One of the first steps in preparing a body for burial was cleansing it with water and then anointing it with oil.) Why do you think Jesus describes Mary's anointing as an act of preparation for his own death?

Notable

Jesus responds to Judas by referring to Deuteronomy 15:11. Though the poor are always present and though serving them is essential, this is an offering given at a particular time for a particular purpose. Jesus defends the woman and her offering, memorializing it forever.

---

4. Smell is incredibly powerful. Particular scents can bring back memories long past and even reignite emotions that accompanied the memories. When the fragrance of Mary's perfume fills the house, what memories do you think it may have brought to mind for the people in the room?

Mary (Luke 10:38–42) . . .

Martha (John 11:20–25) . . .

Lazarus (John 11:43–44) . . .

5. What does Jesus' response reveal about his attitude toward Mary's beautiful gift?

6. When have you found yourself wondering if God is really pleased and delighted in your own gifts and offerings? What encouragement do you find in this passage that God is pleased with you and your gift?

Spend time simply worshiping God. Thank God for who he is and all that he has done in your life. Express your gratitude and adoration.

When Worship Costs More than Expected

John 12–17

From Exodus to Revelation, worship in the Bible is clothed in gold, silver, precious stones, embroidery, robes of gorgeous fabric, bells, and candles.... God ordered beauty, even extravagant beauty in worship, even while His people were still wandering in the desert and living in tents.[10]

—*Anthony Coniaris*

God desires that our relationship with him isn't lived out of a sense of duty as much as out of a sense of devotion. In other words, God longs for us to long for him. In the beauty of his presence, we can't help but find our affections set on God, our hearts captivated by his love. Caught up in the delight of God, powerful feelings of gratitude swell within us and our natural response is worship — words of thanks that roll off the tongue, songs of adoration that spring from the heart, or some other form of praise. When we give back to God, the one who has gifted us with all good things, we reflect his beauty.

When we give a meaningful gift, we often receive the affirming response we anticipated or hoped, but that's not always the case. This is particularly true of a woman who gave a very expensive and beautiful gift to Jesus.

Getting Started: Select One

Experiential Activity: The Scent of Worship

What you'll need:

- ◆ A small bottle of nard, also known as spikenard. You'll find it online by simply Googling the spice, which is commonly bottled as an oil; spikenard may also be found at some local Christian bookstores or retailers that specialize in oils and scented products.

1. Pass around the bottle and invite participants to smell the oil.
2. Discuss the following questions:

   - What one word would you use to describe the scent?
   - Do you find anything about the scent surprising?
   - What do you think it would be like to have an entire bottle poured over your feet?
   - How long do you think the scent might remain on you and everything it touches?

Icebreaker Question

If you're not doing the experiential activity, choose one *of the following sets of questions to begin your discussion.*

- Describe the most meaningful gift you've ever been given. How did the gift make you feel?
- What's the single most meaningful gift you've ever given someone else? How did giving the gift make you feel?
- In what ways does giving gifts reflect God's heart for us?
- What is your all-time favorite scent? What memories does it bring to mind?

Four: When Worship Costs More than Expected

As you watch the DVD, use the following outline to take notes on anything that stands out to you.

In our lives there are moments that we feel compelled to do something extravagant for God, and things don't turn out like we expect.

Jesus had performed many miracles, but raising Lazarus from the dead threatened the religious institutions and Roman Empire like no other.

The beautiful scent poured out, filling the house, permeating everyone's nostrils.

This is a breathtaking portrait of a woman who has been captivated by Jesus and cannot contain it any longer.

Mary is met with contempt for her extravagance.

As we live lives marked by extravagant acts of love, generosity, and worship, we should not be surprised by the critics. If anything, Mary's story teaches us we should expect them.

 ## Group Discussion Questions

(30 – 45 MINUTES)

1. Consider what you learned about this beautiful miracle in the life of Lazarus from the Afterhours personal studies or on the DVD. What caught your attention or stood out most to you?

Captivated by Jesus

2. Read John 12:1 – 11. What do you think compelled Mary to use the alabaster jar in the beautiful way that she did?

> **Notable**
>
> Respectable Jewish women always kept their hair up in public. To allow one's hair to flow freely was the sign of an immoral woman. Despite this cultural taboo, Mary lets down her air with reckless abandon in this beautiful expression of adoration.

3. If you could question Mary about her extravagant and beautiful act, what would you want to know?

How do you imagine Mary's answers to your questions might impact your own relationship with Christ?

4. Read John 11:2. Why do you think Mary is introduced as having anointed the Lord before she actually anoints the Lord in this chapter?

Why do you think John's Gospel adds the detail about Mary wiping Jesus' feet with her hair? What do Mary's actions reveal about her attitude toward Jesus and their relationship?

What Have I Done?

5. What is a contemporary example of an extravagant display that would be comparable to Mary's act?

How might this contemporary example be viewed or even misinterpreted by others?

6. Have you ever given an extravagant gift or act of service to someone or to God and then second-guessed yourself, wondering, *What have I done?* What made you second-guess yourself?

7. This story suggests that extravagant devotion and generosity toward Jesus often will be misunderstood or even criticized. When have you found this to be true in your own life?

8. Are there any areas in which you find yourself quick to question, judge, or criticize those who give God something extravagant?

Quotable

"Like Judas, we may ridicule Mary for her act of extravagance, which costs her a great deal — not only in terms of losing her savings but also in terms of losing face. How impractical! How outlandish and wasteful! But at times authentic worship will appear as impractical, as outlandish and as wasteful as it does here — just like God's grace, which is poured out lavishly on unworthy sinners like Mary, you, and me."[11]

—Paul Louis Metzger

Unable to Hold Back

9. Are there any areas in which you're holding back from offering something extravagant to God because of something that has happened in the past? If so, describe.

10. In what ways has God been extending an invitation to give yourself to him in a greater measure? How can you be more intentional about giving yourself extravagantly and lavishly to God in worship this week?

Mary's beautiful expression of worship didn't just challenge onlookers thousands of years ago but still challenges us today. It invites us to reflect on how we worship, what we sacrifice out of our love for Christ, and what we receive from him in response.

Bonus Activity

To learn more about the artist behind "Autumn Dancers" featured in the introduction of session four, check out Lindsay Hoekstra's site at: *www.lindsayhoekstra.com*.

Close in Prayer

Ask God to:

- Reveal any times when you may have felt disappointment or hurt from a well-intentioned offering.
- Give you God's perspective on your act of worship and heal any areas of hurt.
- Reveal any times when you may have been critical of other people's worship or offering.
- Forgive you.

 ## Jumpstart

To get an insider's look at the Pursuing God series, bonus features, and freebies, as well as join the online discussion, visit *www.pursuinggodbiblestudy.com*.

To prepare for the next group session, read John 18–19 and tackle the After-hours personal studies.

Afterhours Personal Studies

Dive deeper into John's Gospel by engaging in these five personal studies. If you only have time for one, choose Day Five, which will prepare you specifically for the next session.

DAY ONE: Entering Jerusalem

John 12:12–50

After raising Lazarus from the dead and being anointed by Mary for his own burial, Jesus now makes his triumphant entry into Jerusalem. The much-anticipated Messiah arrives, and crowds of eager worshipers greet him by crying out, "Hosanna!" The word *Hosanna* can be translated "Save us!" or "Give us salvation now!" The shouts of those in the crowds echo the words of Psalm 118:26.

The crowds also greet Jesus with palm branches in their hands. These branches were often used as part of the processions at the Feast of Tabernacles as well as to display Jewish patriotism. The people's use of palm branches to announce Jesus' arrival in Jerusalem suggests they were ready to accept him as the long-awaited Messiah, their king.

1. Read John 12:12–19. What do the details of Jesus' entry disclose about the way he is revealing himself as the Messiah? (*Hint:* See Zechariah 9:9 and Psalm 118:26.)

2. Read John 12:20–36. Why do you think Jesus goes to such great lengths to point people toward glorifying God? (*Hint:* See John 8:54; 13:31; 14:13.)

Think back over the last day or two. In what ways did your words, thoughts, or actions bring glory to God?

If you have trouble thinking of an example, consider any missed opportunities you may have had. How might you use a similar situation to glorify God in the future?

3. The world views death as the end, the ultimate loss, but through Scripture we see death as a new beginning and something through which we gain even more intimate access to God. What does Jesus specifically teach us about his death in this passage?

> **Notable**
>
> John often uses the word *hour* to refer to the time of Jesus' crucifixion (i.e., John 12:23).

4. Read John 12:37–50. John's Gospel draws on Isaiah 6:10 and Isaiah 53:1 to explain how our hearts are hardened toward God. What happens to a person's spiritual senses when he or she refuses to obey or honor God?

Are there any areas or relationships in your family, community, church, or workplace where you've become hardhearted?

5. Religious leaders and others in Jesus' day lived for the praise of people rather than the praise of God (John 12:43). In what ways have you been tempted to love the praise of people more than the praise of God?

6. Even after all of the rejection and criticism, Jesus still invites people to embrace the light, reject the darkness, and listen to his voice. Jesus invites people to eternal life. Jesus longs to restore the relationship between people and God if they will simply respond to the invitation. What does this reveal about Jesus' heart for people?

In what ways do you recognize Jesus' unending invitation in your own life?

Spend some time asking God to reveal any areas in your life where your heart has grown hard toward him. Ask God to soften your heart and allow the power of his truth to transform you.

DAY TWO: **The Last Supper**

John 13

Before the Passover, Jesus shares an unforgettable meal with his followers in which he both washes their feet and exposes the one who will betray him. Through John 13 and the upcoming handful of chapters, we're given the opportunity to listen in on an intimate conversation between Jesus and his closest followers as well as watch how he interacts with them. These are some of the most tender and beautiful exchanges between Jesus and his disciples.

1. Read John 13:1 – 20. What does the passage reveal about why Jesus took on the duties of a slave or servant — washing the disciples' feet — during their final hours together?

How does Jesus' act of washing the disciples' feet demonstrate the attitude he wants us to have toward others?

In what situation or relationship is it most challenging for you right now to consider humbling yourself as a way of serving others?

Notable

John's account of the Last Supper differs from the other Gospels. John notes the final supper is the night *before* instead of the night *of* the Passover. John doesn't mention the securing or preparation of the upper room, but includes the scene of the foot washing as well as the account of Judas' betrayal. In addition, John lacks the Eucharistic language or detailed description of Holy Communion found in the other Gospels.

2. When it comes to having a servant heart, how would you describe your behavior toward various people in your life: for example, your family; people you know at school, work, or in your daily activities; members of your church or small group; your neighborhood or community? Place an X on the following continuums to indicate your response.

    With my family, I behave like ...

    A HUMBLE SERVANT   ROYALTY

With people I know at school, work, or in my daily activities, I behave like ...

_____

A HUMBLE SERVANT   ROYALTY

With people in my church or small group, I behave like ...

_____

A HUMBLE SERVANT   ROYALTY

With people in my neighborhood or community, I behave like ...

_____

A HUMBLE SERVANT   ROYALTY

As you review your responses on the continuums, how would you describe the degree to which your relationships demonstrate a servant heart?

3. Although we can't go around offering to wash the feet of everyone we know, we can make small decisions every day to serve others. What equivalents of foot washing might you practice with the people in your life? Write down one or two ideas for each group listed below.

In my home or with extended family members ...

In my school, workplace, or other daily activities ...

In my church or small group ...

In my neighborhood or community ...

4. Read John 13:21–38. Why do you think Jesus selected Judas as a disciple when he knew Judas would pilfer money and eventually betray him?

5. Jesus says that people will know we are his disciples by our love for one another (John 13:35). Think back over the last day or two. In what ways have you struggled with the command to love one another?

Spend some time asking God to expand your heart for service. Ask for a special sensitivity to those around you who are in need as well as for wisdom in how to respond with the love of God.

DAY THREE: Final Words of Comfort

John 14–15

One can only imagine what Judas felt as he looked into Jesus' eyes as the Son of God tenderly washed between his toes. Only a few moments later, Jesus dismisses Judas from dinner to do what he had been planning for some time — betray his rabbi. The rest of the disciples finish the meal listening to Jesus' words of comfort and challenge.

1. Read John 14:1–31. How does Jesus comfort his followers throughout this passage? How do Jesus' words comfort you?

Scripture	How does Jesus comfort his followers?	How do Jesus' words comfort you?
John 14:1–4	*Example: He instructs his disciples not to be troubled and assures them that he is preparing a place for them.*	*Example: God is also preparing a place for me!*
John 14:12–13		
John 14:16		
John 14:18		
John 14:27		
John 14:29		

One of the most important sources of comfort to the disciples is the Holy Spirit—who is called Counselor (or Helper, NASB) in John 14:16, 26. Jesus promises that the Holy Spirit will help the disciples to remember all that he taught them (v. 26). Remembering was an important facet of faith throughout the Old Testament as well. People were to remember the words God spoke to them in the past. Some even built pillars or rock altars to commemorate God's activity among them.

2. How do memories of God's past activity in your life impact your ability to trust God in the present?

After describing himself as the way, truth, and life (John 14:6), Jesus goes on to reveal himself as the true vine (John 15:1). Since, according to John14:31, Jesus had left the upper room, some scholars believe that when Jesus delivered his teaching on the vines he was either near the golden vine image that decorated the main entrance of the temple or in a nearby field where vines were planted.

3. Read John 15:1–11. *Abide* means "to remain, continue, stay; to have one's abode, dwell, reside; or continue in a particular condition, attitude, or relationship."[12] Jesus commands his disciples to "remain [abide] in me" (John 15:4) rather than commanding them to be fruitful. Which is more challenging for you—to abide in Christ or to do good works for Christ? Why?

4. Read John 15:12–27. Most of us won't be required to literally lay down our lives for someone we love, but we can choose to make personal sacrifices for the sake of others. How has a friend or family member laid down his or her life for you by putting your needs first?

   How did this sacrifice impact you and your relationship with this person?

5. How have you laid down your life for someone else recently by putting his or her needs first?

How did your sacrifice impact the other person and your relationship with that person?

Spend some time praying about what it looks like for you to abide in Jesus in the midst of your daily schedule and routine. Ask God for the strength and grace to dwell or reside in Christ.

DAY FOUR: Jesus' Final Promise and Prayer
John 16–17

Jesus continues to inform the disciples about what's going to happen so they aren't caught unaware. The disciples should anticipate hostility from the religious establishment but also know that God's Spirit is with them even in the midst of fiery trials.

1. Read John 16:1–15. This passage teaches that the Holy Spirit convicts the world of three things—sin, righteousness, and judgment. How does each of these convictions reveal Jesus as the Messiah, the Son of God? How have you experienced each conviction of the Holy Spirit in your own life?

How the Holy Spirit convicts the world	How this conviction reveals Jesus as the Messiah	How I have experienced this conviction of the Holy Spirit in my life
Sin		
Righteousness		
Judgment		

2. How is the promised work of the Holy Spirit explained differently in John 16:13–15 than John 14:26?

   How have you experienced the Holy Spirit working in your own life?

3. Read John 16:16–33. Why do you think the disciples were confused by Jesus' use of the phrase "a little while" (vv. 16–17)?

   The disciples became more concerned with the timing of the promise than the promise itself. In what ways do believers today get distracted by the timing of God's promises rather than the actual promises?

   In what ways do you find yourself distracted by the timing of God's promises rather than the actual promises?

In John 16:31 (NASB), Jesus asks, "Do you now believe?" His question highlights a message reiterated throughout John's Gospel. The book was written so that people would believe. Now Jesus himself is asking the question, "Do you now believe?" Jesus then proceeds to pray for himself and his disciples.

4. Read John 17:1–26. What is the one request Jesus makes for himself (v. 1)?

Why do you think Jesus makes this request?

Notable

Moses (Numbers 11:15), Elijah (1 Kings 19:4), and Jonah (Jonah 4:3, 8) all asked God to take them out of the world. God denied all of their requests. In John 17:15, Jesus prays that his disciples would not be taken from the world, but remain in it — set apart as God's people and protected from the evil one.

5. What does Jesus' prayer reveal about his desire for his followers — including you?

6. On the evening of Jesus' arrest, he does not pray for immediate concerns but long-term issues that his disciples will face in the future. Do you tend to pray for immediate concerns or long-term concerns? Place an X on the continuum below to describe your response.

I PRAY FOR IMMEDIATE
CONCERNS.

I PRAY FOR LONG-TERM
CONCERNS.

If a balanced prayer life includes having a conversation with God about both immediate and long-term concerns, what kinds of things would be on your prayer list? Write three or four items in each column below.

My immediate concerns	My long-term concerns

Spend some time asking God to increase your awareness of the presence of the Holy Spirit in your life as both a source of conviction and a source of comfort.

DAY FIVE: A Double Betrayal

John 18:1–27

Judas is the name most of us think of first when it comes to Jesus' betrayal. John's Gospel reveals in detail that not one but two of Jesus' disciples betrayed him. John 18 places the accounts back to back, providing a setting to compare the two betrayals and how each betrayer responded.

> **Notable**
>
> In John 18:4–5 (NASB), Jesus asks the Roman cohort and religious leaders, "Whom do you seek?" "Jesus of Nazareth," they answer. Jesus replies, "I am he" — a statement reflective of the many "I am" statements found throughout John that reveal Jesus' relationship with God.

1. Read John 18:1 – 11. What do you think the disciples first thought when they saw Judas with the Roman cohort and religious leaders carrying lanterns, torches, and weapons?

   If you had been among the disciples, what would have been your reaction?

   What do you imagine ran through Jesus' mind when he saw Judas?

2. Read Matthew 26:47 – 50. How does Matthew's account of Jesus' betrayal differ from John's? What does each writer emphasize about Judas' betrayal?

3. Read Matthew 27:1 – 10. After the betrayal, Judas feels remorse. How does he handle the remorse?

   Do you think the story of Judas had to end the way it did? Why or why not?

Notable

According to John 18:6, when Jesus said, "I am he," the soldiers fell to the ground. This is reminiscent of scenes throughout the Old Testament where people responded to the power and revelation of God by falling on their faces (Genesis 17:3; Joshua 5:14; Ezekiel 1:28).

4. Read John 18:12–27. How is Peter's betrayal of Jesus similar to and different from Judas' betrayal?

In your own life, have you ever betrayed Jesus? How did your betrayal impact your relationship with Christ?

5. Read John 21:15–21. Why do you think Jesus goes out of his way to speak to Peter and remind him of his purpose, calling, and future?

6. What insights can you learn from Judas and Peter about sin and temptation in your life?

What insights can you learn from Judas and Peter about redemption and restoration in your life?

Spend some time prayerfully asking God to reveal ways in which you have either betrayed or denied the work of God in your life. Ask for forgiveness as well as the grace to walk in faithfulness.

Mistakes that Refine Instead of Define

John 18–19

> Moral principles are vital, yet so often we have to drive ourselves to do what is right. Beauty, on the other hand, haunts us. It draws and compels and gives.... I might respond to God as a great commander-in-chief but I could not give myself to him as the goal of all my longing and my supreme delight.[13]
>
> —*Richard Harries*

Just because God is beautiful and God is perfect does not mean that God's beauty can only be reflected in perfection. Rather, God showcases the beauty of his work on broken and imperfect canvases. Some of God's most beautiful work is on display in the lives of those whose pasts are most messed up, whose situations seemed beyond repair.

We all have circumstances and situations in life that we look back on and think, *I wish I had handled things differently. I wish had been more honest. I wish I had been more courageous. I wish I had been the one to speak up.* Yet the question we must all face is whether we will allow our mistakes to *define* us or to *refine* us.

As we submit ourselves to God's work in our lives we can find that our weaknesses and failures become places for the glory of God to infuse, heal, and invite us into wholeness.

Getting Started: Select One

Experiential Activity: The Many Faces of Failure

What you'll need:

- ◆ Humorous and engaging photos or images that portray failure
- ◆ Photocopies of the images, or a laptop and video projector to display the images

1. Visit *www.failblog.org*, a website that allows people to upload images of various failures — many of which are failures in communication. (*Note:* Since this website is open to anyone uploading photos, be aware that some language and images may not be appropriate for distributing in the group. Discretion advised.)
2. Select four or five humorous, engaging, and thought-provoking failure images and print them out.
3. Pass the images around the group.
4. Discuss the following questions:

   - What does each image reveal about the person who failed?
   - Do you find the failure funny? Why or why not?
   - Which failure causes you to have the most compassion on the person who failed? Why?

Icebreaker Question

If you're not doing the experiential activity, choose one *of the following sets of questions to begin your discussion.*

- If you had one do-over in an area of your life — professional, relational, or spiritual — what would you choose?
- What tends to be your response to personal failure? How does your response change when it's someone else who has failed?
- Use your imagination for a moment. If you had the opportunity to ask the disciple Peter, "What is your most regrettable moment?" how do you think he would answer?

Five: Mistakes that Refine Instead of Define

As you watch the DVD, use the following outline to take notes on anything that stands out to you.

Why didn't I speak up?

Once Christ is arrested, we get a different glimpse of Peter.

Jesus is questioned by the authorities and denies nothing, while Peter is questioned by strangers and denies everything.

On that morning, Peter felt defeated not by armies or authorities, but by himself.

Peter's denial of Jesus does not define him; it refined him.

I can't go back and make things happen in a different way than they did in that room with those religious leaders that day. But I can go forward.

Group Discussion Questions

1. Consider what you learned about this beautiful portrait of restoration in the life of Peter from the Afterhours personal studies or on the DVD. What caught your attention or stood out most to you?

Why Didn't I Speak Up?

2. Have you ever been in a situation where you wish you had spoken up about your faith but instead remained silent? Briefly describe the situation and why you chose not to say anything.

If you could go back into that situation and say something, what would you say?

3. Read John 18:12 – 27. Why do you think Peter didn't speak up and admit to being a follower of Jesus?

Mistakes that Define

4. What emotions do you think Peter felt when he heard the sound of a rooster announcing the dawn of a new day?

Which of those emotions can you relate to in your own moments of failure?

Notable

All four Gospels agree that one of the challenges to Peter came
from a slave girl. In other words, Peter denied his faith to someone who posed no threat to him. The strength and fervor in
Peter's previous declaration that he would lay down his own life
for Jesus (John 13:37) stand in stark contrast to denying Jesus
to a slave girl at night.

5. Read Luke 22:54–62. How does Luke's account of Peter's denial differ from John's account?

6. Luke describes Jesus turning and looking at Peter (Luke 22:61). What do you think was communicated to Peter through that glance?

Mistakes that Refine

7. Pair up with another person. Take turns reading aloud to each other the passages listed on the chart that follows. After each passage, briefly discuss what it teaches about how God looks at our failures and mistakes and how this truth encourages you. Briefly note your responses in the space provided.

Scripture	What it teaches about how God looks at our failures and mistakes	How this truth encourages me
Psalm 73:26		
Romans 8:1–2		
Romans 8:35–39		
1 John 1:9		
John 21:15–22		

8. How would you describe the difference between being *defined* by a failure and being *refined* by a failure?

9. What role does God play in the difference between being refined versus being defined by a mistake?

10. How have you seen God play a role in your own life when it comes to being refined rather than defined by a mistake?

We all can look back on times when we wish we had responded differently. Though we can't go back and change the past, we can move forward. We are given countless opportunities not only to share our faith but to live it out, bearing witness to God's redemption.

Bonus Activity

To learn more about the artist behind "Solo" featured in the introduction of session five, check out David Warmenhoven's site at: *www.warmenhovenart.blogspot.com*.

Close in Prayer

Ask God to:

- Reveal any moments from the past that may have defined you instead of refined you to become more Christlike.
- Make you receptive to the Holy Spirit's work, especially in areas of your life that need to be illuminated by truth or experience healing.
- Give you the courage to respond differently in areas where you have failed in the past.

 ## Jumpstart

To get an insider's look at the Pursuing God series, bonus features, and free-bies, as well as join the online discussion, visit *www.pursuinggodbiblestudy.com*.

To prepare for the next group session, read John 20:1–18 and tackle the Afterhours personal studies.

Afterhours Personal Studies

Dive deeper into John's Gospel by engaging in these five personal studies. If you only have time for one, choose Day Five, which will prepare you specifically for the next session.

DAY ONE: Standing Trial Unjustly

John 18:12–40

Jesus is given two different trials. He stands before both Jewish and Roman judges. John's Gospel is the only one to mention that Jesus appears before Annas. Why does he go before Annas when it's his son-in-law, Caiaphas, who actually holds the position of high priest? Some scholars believe that because the appointment for high priest was for life (Numbers 35:25), Annas may have been seen as the real high priest or the one with more experience, age, and authority.

Jesus is questioned in an informal manner. Jewish law required witnesses to be present in a formal trial, but since none are mentioned, the questioning is probably not official. The turn of events suggests that the case should have been dismissed as a mistrial, but instead a series of events lead to Jesus' execution.

1. Read John 18:12–24. What does Jesus reveal when questioned about his disciples and teaching?

    Why do you think one of the officers strikes Jesus? (*Hint:* See Exodus 22:28.)

John's Gospel only briefly mentions that Annas sent Jesus to Caiaphas, the high priest of the year. Before Jesus could stand before a Roman court, the charges against him had to be made by the official Jewish priest. Only then is Jesus taken into the headquarters of the Romans to stand trial before Pilate.

Jews who walked into the house of any Gentile were deemed unclean and unable to celebrate the Passover. Thus, the Jews refused to walk into the Praetorium where Jesus stood trial before the Roman ruler Pilate.

> **Notable**
>
> Barabbas' name can be translated as "son of the father." This phrase parallels the way John's Gospel describes Jesus throughout the text. The people literally chose between two different sons of the father.

2. Do you think it's hypocritical that the Jewish leaders refuse to enter the Praetorium? Why or why not?

3. Read John 18:25 – 40. What is Pilate's overall response to the religious leaders' charges against Jesus?

How does Pilate try to set Jesus free? Why do his efforts fail?

John's Gospel repeatedly uses the word *king* to describe Jesus. In fact, when Jesus calls his first disciples (John 1:49), Nathanael makes the initial declaration that Jesus is not only the Son of God, but the king of Israel. In the sixth chapter of John, when Jesus perceives the people are going to come and take him by force in order to instate him as king, he retreats to a quiet mountainside. When Jesus enters Jerusalem on a donkey, he is greeted with the title "king of Israel."

4. Jesus' kingship is questioned and mocked throughout his arrest, trial, and crucifixion. Why do you think Pilate called Jesus "the king of the Jews" when requesting his release (v. 39)?

Why would the Jewish people react so negatively to this title for Jesus?

5. What in this passage suggests that God is fully in control throughout Jesus' trials?

Jesus' trial is marked by injustice. No witnesses provide testimony of Jesus' guilt nor does Caiaphas. Though the Jews call Jesus a criminal, there's not any proof. Pilate finds no basis of a crime that Jesus has committed. Yet despite all this, Jesus is found guilty based on nothing more than political maneuvering.

6. What types of situations make you question whether God is fully in control?

What does it mean for you to trust God or commit yourself to God's care even in the midst of life's most severe trials?

Spend time reflecting on areas of your life that feel completely out of control. Ask God to give you grace, strength, and faith in these areas and to wholly trust that God is in control.

DAY TWO: Innocent Punishable by Death

John 19:1–15

Following Jesus' trial, Pilate decides to have Jesus scourged and then to release him in the hope that this will appease the Jews. In addition to the scourging, the soldiers seem to take pleasure in harassing Jesus.

1. Read John 19:1–3. How do the soldiers mock Jesus?

   Why do you think the soldiers were so committed to humiliating Jesus?

2. Read John 19:4–15. How does Pilate's approach and attitude toward Jesus differ from that of the soldiers?

3. How would you describe the Jews' attitude toward Jesus?

4. Briefly review your responses to questions 1–3. How do you see the attitudes of Pilate, the soldiers, and the Jews demonstrated in people's attitudes toward Jesus today?

   Pilate...

   The soldiers...

   The Jews...

   In what ways, if any, have these attitudes sometimes characterized your own response to Jesus?

5. In what areas of your own life have you discovered your heart becoming hard toward God? Toward others?

Spend some time in prayer reflecting on your attitude toward God. Ask the Holy Spirit to illuminate any areas where God wants to soften your heart.

John's account of Jesus' death differs from the other Gospels. Details are specifically chosen to highlight certain beliefs, moods, and relationships. Instead of a cry on the cross asking why God has forsaken him, Jesus declares that it's finished. This portrait suggests that Jesus is in control from beginning to end. Jesus is not being forced to die; he is choosing to give up his own life.

The Gospel of John testifies that Jesus is given over to the Jews to be crucified and forced to carry his own cross to the place of his execution. Pilate writes an inscription for Jesus that declared "Jesus the Nazarene, the King of the Jews" in three different languages so that all who could read would understand. The religious leaders protest the inscription, but Pilate refuses to make any adjustments or to take it down.

1. Look up the following passages and write down Jesus' final words from each crucifixion account:

Scripture	Jesus' final words
Matthew 27:33–50	
Mark 15:22–41	
Luke 23:33–49	
John 19:16–30	

2. Which of Jesus' statements impacts you the most? Why?

3. What do Jesus' statements reveal about Jesus' identity and mission?

Notable

Jesus' final cry — "It is finished" — in John's Gospel are not words of concession or defeat, but a powerful declaration that Jesus has triumphantly fulfilled his mission.

4. Why do you think John's Gospel notes that Jesus expressed concern for his mother?

What do you think Mary felt as she watched these events unfold (Luke 2:19)?

Quotable

"Therefore I will give him a portion among the great, and he will divide the spoils with the strong, because he poured out his life unto death, and was numbered with the transgressors. For he bore the sin of many, and made intercession for the transgressors."

—Isaiah 53:12

5. In what ways was Jesus dead to the things of this world long before he ever hung on a cross?

6. In what area of your life might God be calling you to take up your cross and die to your own desires?

The prospect of dying to anything can be frightening, but death always precedes new life. What new life do you hope might emerge from accepting God's invitation to die to yourself?

Spend some time asking God to give you the strength to respond with a sense of joy and expectation to anything God may be calling you to die to.

DAY FOUR: Jesus' Burial

John 19:31–42

The Romans often allowed the corpse of a person who had been crucified to remain on the cross until it was devoured by birds and wild animals. But the Jews did not want bodies to remain on the cross for the holy day, so they sped along their removal. The soldiers break the legs of a criminal being executed alongside Jesus so he can no longer lift himself up to breathe. Noting that Jesus is dead, they leave his bones unbroken. To confirm Jesus' death, a soldier pierces his body with a spear. The Scripture notes that blood and water flowed as a result (John 19:34).

1. Read John 19:31–42. Why is the detail of Jesus' bones remaining unbroken so significant? (*Hint:* See Exodus 12:46; Numbers 9:12; Psalm 34:20.)

Notable

Some scholars believe the water and blood that burst from Jesus' side are symbolic of the Lord's Supper (blood) and baptism (water).

After Jesus' body is removed from the cross, Joseph of Arimathea suddenly appears and disappears from John's Gospel. The one act he is known for is caring for Jesus' body. Though many followers flee after Jesus' death, Joseph courageously steps forward to ask for the remains.

2. What do the following passages reveal about Joseph of Arimathea?

Passage	Joseph of Arimathea
Mark 15:43	
Luke 23:50	
Matthew 27:57	

In what ways, if any, have you tried to keep your relationship with Jesus a secret as Joseph of Arimathea did two thousand years ago?

3. Does Nicodemus' appearance in John 19 surprise you? Why or why not?

4. What does Nicodemus' appearance suggest that he now believes (following his initial meeting with Jesus at night in John 3)?

5. In your own spiritual life, would you describe yourself as a daytime follower (like the disciples) or a nighttime follower like Nicodemus? Explain.

Spend some time asking God to give you more courage to express and share your faith in your everyday life.

DAY FIVE: **An Empty Tomb and an Unlikely Witness**

John 20:1–18

Though Joseph of Arimathea and Nicodemus provide a tomb and spices for the body, one can only imagine the pain and anguish, confusion and fear all the followers of Jesus feel following his death. The source of their hope is gone. Now what?

John's Gospel describes an unlikely character by the name of Mary Magdalene approaching the tomb. The only other time John's Gospel mentions Mary Magdalene is John 19:25 when she appears at the cross.

1. Read John 20:1–18 and then look up the passages listed below. What does each one reveal about Mary Magdalene?

Scripture	Mary Magdalene
Matthew 27:55–56	
Mark 15:40–41	
Luke 8:1–3	

Notable

Stealing a body was considered a horrible offense in Jewish culture. Emperor Claudius eventually made grave robbing a capital crime punishable by death.

2. Why do you think that of all the people Jesus could have revealed himself to after the resurrection he chose to reveal himself to Mary Magdalene?

What might this reveal about Jesus' mission and identity?

3. John's Gospel notes details about how the linens from Jesus' body were discovered. What do the linens (vv. 6–7) suggest about the scene and what may have happened to Jesus' body?

4. Of all of the questions Jesus could have asked Mary Magdalene, why do you think that he asks her, "Who is it you are looking for?"

What does the first thing Mary Magdalene says when she recognizes Jesus reveal about her relationship with Jesus?

5. Scholars debate why Jesus told Mary Magdalene not to hold onto him. Some believe Jesus is telling Mary to let go of him so she can go and tell the disciples. Others suggest that Jesus is telling Mary that she can't hold onto Jesus in his current form, because he has yet to come again. The relationship is changing and Mary can't cling to the past. Still others suggest that Jesus is instructing Mary to let go of him in his physical form because Jesus is going to send the Holy Spirit. Why do you think Jesus told Mary Magdalene not to hold onto him?

What do you think Jesus was trying to communicate?

What would your reaction have been if Jesus had revealed himself to you as he did to Mary?

6. What is your response to the risen Christ?

Who is the first person that comes to mind when you think about sharing the good news of Christ's resurrection with someone?

Spend time reflecting on John 20:1 – 18. Prayerfully imagine what it would be like to be the first person to the tomb. What would you expect to see and encounter? What would be your response to the risen Christ? Thank Jesus not only for his sacrifice but for the resurrection. Ask God to make the resurrection even more alive in your own heart.

The Hope and Healing of Resurrection

John 20–21

> In one of the New Testament's greatest claims, the kingdoms of this world are to be-come the kingdom of God, so the beauty of this world will be enfolded in the beauty of God — and not just the beauty of God himself, but the beauty which, because God is the creator par excellence, he will create when the present world is rescued, healed, restored, and completed.[16]
>
> —N. T. Wright

Of all the portraits of Jesus throughout John's Gospel, perhaps none is more stunning than the resurrection. This moment invites us to believe that Jesus is who he said he was — the very Son of God who walked the earth, laid down his life, and returned to the Father. The resurrection is an invitation to embrace the beauty of God through the person of Jesus by believing in him.

Throughout the Gospel of John, we see again and again that Jesus knows his mission. At times, he hints to his followers about "the hour" of his death. At other times, Jesus takes a much more direct route in preparing his disciples for the events that are about to unfold. Even in his arrest, trial, and crucifixion, Jesus displays that he is who he has said he's been all along. Jesus' death is not the end of the story!

(10 – 15 MINUTES)

Experiential Activity: Images of the Resurrection

What you'll need:
- ◆ Well-known and/or unknown images of the resurrection
- ◆ Photocopies of the images, or a laptop and video projector to display the images

1. Google "famous resurrection artwork" to find images of the resurrection. One site that is helpful is *www.bible-art.info/resurrection.htm*. Consider looking at Rembrandt's *The Resurrection*, El Greco's *The Resurrection*, and Frederick Hart's *Christ Rising*, among others.
2. Pass the images around the group.
3. Discuss the following questions:

   - Which image do you find most compelling? Why?
   - What mood did the artist capture?
   - What emotions are conveyed through each person's expression?
   - What does the artwork communicate about Jesus' relationship to his followers and his relationship to God?

Icebreaker Question

If you're not doing the experiential activity, choose one *of the following sets of questions to begin your discussion.*

- Have you ever celebrated Lent — the forty days before Easter devoted to penitence, prayer, and self-denial — in order to prepare for the resurrection? If so, describe your experience and what you learned.
- Other than Easter, what seasons or situations remind you of the resurrection of Jesus? Why is it important to reflect on the resurrection in your own spiritual journey?
- Have you ever visited the Holy Land? If so, what was your most meaningful experience? If you haven't visited the Holy Land but were given the opportunity, where is the one place you'd want to go? Why?

Six: The Hope and Healing of Resurrection

As you watch the DVD, use the following outline to take notes on anything that stands out to you.

Stepping inside the tomb, dark and cold, I was struck by the fact there's no one there.

The disciples head back home to try to wrap their minds and hearts around all they've seen and experienced. Mary just sits by the tomb.

The Son of God who created the skies, formed the mountains, and unleashed the solar system, is now mistaken for a gardener.

Sometimes all it takes is one word from God and everything changes.

The invitation to know Jesus is an invitation to believe in him.

The same power of God that raised Jesus from the dead isn't what was but what is.

Group Discussion Questions

1. Based on the DVD teaching or the Afterhours personal studies, what have you learned from the beautiful portrait of resurrection in the life of Jesus and his encounters after he rose from the dead? What caught your attention or stood out most to you?

> **Notable**
>
> The Gospel of John's account of the resurrection is different than any of the other Gospels. John's Gospel tells stories others do not and omits stories that others tell, but still celebrates the resurrection and morning discovery of the empty tomb.

2. What range of emotions do you think Jesus' followers experienced after his death and before the resurrection? What emotions would you experience if you were in the same situation?

The Resurrection Power of Jesus

3. Read John 20:1–18. What is significant about Mary Magdalene being the first person to discover an empty tomb? What is John's Gospel trying to communicate about the relationship between Jesus and women?

> **Notable**
>
> A woman's testimony was not considered evidence in court. Only men's testimonies were considered. Jesus tells Mary — a woman whose testimony doesn't count — to go tell the disciples of Jesus' resurrection. The very first evangelist of the risen Christ is a woman! John's Gospel esteems women and the role they play as children of God.

4. Throughout the Gospel of John, many people have misinterpreted Jesus' teachings and identity.

- Jesus' body is misinterpreted as an earthly temple (John 2:20).
- Nicodemus misinterprets what it means to be born again or from above (John 3:4).
- The woman at the well misinterprets Jesus' promise of living water (John 4:13–14).
- Spiritual food is confused with regular food (John 4:33).
- Receiving Christ's Spirit is confused with eating Jesus' body and drinking Jesus' blood (John 6:52).
- Jesus' leaving is misinterpreted as Jesus killing himself (John 8:22).
- Spiritual bondage is misinterpreted as physical slavery (John 8:33).

What misunderstanding have you had in the past about God? What opened your eyes or ears to understanding?

A Change in Perspective

5. With one word Jesus breaks through Mary's grief-induced fog and enables her to see what's really going on. Have you ever sensed God communicating to you in a way that changed everything? If so, describe.

How does God most often break through your spiritual fog (for example: in the details of daily life, in spiritual conversations with others, through personal Bible study or prayer, etc.)?

6. Read John 20:19–31. Use your creative imagination. Where do you think Thomas was when Jesus appeared to the others? (*Note:* Be creative and even humorous in your answers—such as he was out fishing for the big one!)

Thomas spent years with Jesus witnessing miracles and listening to teaching, yet he refuses to believe. What are some things about God that are still hard for you to believe or wrap your mind around?

Quotable

"The empty tomb never resists honest investigation. A lobotomy is not a prerequisite of discipleship. Following Christ demands faith, but not blind faith. 'Come and see,' the angel invites. Shall we?"[17]
—Max Lucado

7. Jesus' appearance after the resurrection is consistent with all he has promised, taught, and declared. What changes about being a follower of Jesus Christ after the resurrection?

The Call to Believe

8. In John 20:30–31, we are reminded of the purpose of John's Gospel. It's written so that people will believe that Jesus is the Christ. How has this study of John's Gospel impacted your view of Jesus or your relationship with Jesus?

9. In what area of your life do you most long for new life?

   How do you imagine things might change if you could experience the resurrection power of Christ in this area of your life?

10. As you reflect on the last six sessions you've spent studying John's Gospel, what have been some of the most meaningful insights or echoes that God has been speaking to you?

The empty tomb and the resurrection power of Christ calls us to life— whole, abundant life. Through his death, resurrection, and promise of imminent return we have the opportunity to live in a vibrant relationship with Jesus.

Bonus Activity

To learn more about the artist behind "For the Joy Set before Him" featured in the introduction of session six, check out Alexis Wilson's site at: *www.alexis-art.com.*

Close in Prayer

Ask God to:

- Reveal the resurrection power in your life.
- Unleash healing and restoration into every area of life—including broken relationships, work situations, financial challenges, health struggles, etc.
- Draw people into the wonder of God's beauty in the person of Jesus Christ.

 ## Jumpstart

To get an insider's look at the Pursuing God series, bonus features, and freebies, as well as join the online discussion, visit *www.pursuinggodbiblestudy.com*.

Tackle the Afterhours personal studies and consider organizing a final gathering for your group to connect, share a meal, and hang out. If you enjoyed this study, consider another six-week DVD study in this series called *Pursuing God's Love: Stories from the Book of Genesis*, which invites people to dig deeper into God's Word and explore this foundational book of the Bible.

Afterhours Personal Studies

Dive deeper into John's Gospel by engaging in these five personal studies.

DAY ONE: A Surprise Appearance among the Disciples
John 20:19–31

Behind locked doors, the disciples are huddled together. Mary Magdalene has answered countless questions about what she saw, heard, and experienced at the garden tomb. Some of the disciples are probably wondering if what she said really happened. Simon Peter and another disciple (most likely John) confirmed the body was missing, but they never saw Jesus. Yet something about the passion and details of Mary Magdalene's story makes them want to believe it's true.

1. Read John 20:19–30. How does Jesus greet the disciples?

   In what ways is this greeting consistent with Jesus' mission and identity? (*Hint:* See John 14:27 and 16:33.)

2. Why does Jesus breathe on the disciples?

What biblical images come to mind when you reflect on this scene? (*Hint:* See Genesis 2:7, John 1:33; John 3:34; John 14:17.)

> ### Notable
> John doesn't use the noun *faith* (Greek: *pistis*) in his Gospel, but uses the verb *to believe* (Greek: *pisteuo*) almost a hundred times. John's Gospel remains focused on inviting readers to believe in Jesus.

3. Do you think Thomas' demand to see and touch Jesus' wounds is reasonable? Why or why not?

   In what ways are Thomas' demands still prevalent today?

4. Why do you think Jesus reappears to the disciples and addresses Thomas' struggle with faith?

   What does this reveal about Jesus' promise to make sure none are lost?

5. Jesus pursues Thomas. He specifically reveals himself to Thomas, inviting Thomas to touch his scars. In what ways has Jesus been pursuing you over the course of this study?

6. What evidence or reasoning convinces you to believe that Jesus rose from the dead?

What does the resurrection mean to you personally? How does your view of the resurrection impact your relationship with Christ?

Spend some time reflecting on the ways in which Jesus has personally made himself real to you. Ask Jesus to continue revealing himself to you in very personal, real, and meaningful ways that strengthen your faith. Keep an eye and ear open for the ways he may answer that prayer during the upcoming week.

DAY TWO: Jesus Hosts Breakfast on the Beach
John 21:1–14

In the final chapter of the Gospel of John, Jesus appears unexpectedly to his disciples after a long night of fishing. There's something tender about this beautiful scene of Jesus meeting his disciples right where they are — on the edge of the lake — in order to share a meal.

1. Read John 21:1 – 14. In the midst of so much uncertainty, why do you think Peter decides to return to fishing?

What do you return to when you face uncertainty in your own life?

2. What does Peter's response to hearing "it is the Lord" (vv. 7–8) reveal about Peter's own desire to know and follow Jesus?

3. The meal Jesus provides the disciples is not new to them. Where else has Jesus eaten the same meal with his followers? (*Hint:* See John 6:1–14.)

What memories do you think this meal invokes in the disciples?

4. The mention of a charcoal fire is only found in one other place in the New Testament. What happened the last time Peter found himself standing in front of a charcoal fire? (*Hint:* See John 18:18 NASB.)

5. Read Luke 5:1–11. What parallels do you see between the accounts of Jesus approaching the disciples on the lake of Gennesaret early in his ministry and Jesus approaching the disciples on the lake of Tiberias after the resurrection?

6. In what ways are you allowing Jesus to meet you where you are in your life right now?

Spend some time asking God to meet you right where you are in your relationships, personal life, and daily responsibilities. Be expectant for God's presence in your life.

DAY THREE: Jesus Challenges Peter

After an unforgettable breakfast with Jesus on the beach, Jesus focuses on Peter. Just as Peter denied Jesus three times after his arrest, Jesus now reinstates Peter by asking him three questions.

1. Read John 21:15–25. Jesus asks Peter, "Do you truly love me more than these?" Considering the scene, what do you think "these" refers to?

Notable

There are multiple words for "love" in Greek — two of which are *agape* and *phileo*. *Agape* expresses an unconditional, sacrificial love (like that of Christ for us). *Phileo* is a friendship-type love (think Phil-adelphia).

2. How does Jesus connect love and service in his interaction with Peter? How are love of God and service of God connected in your own faith journey?

3. How does Jesus give Peter a second chance?

What from the origins of Peter's name gives insight into Peter's purpose for the church? (*Hint:* See John 1:42.)

In what ways has God extended a second chance to you?

4. How does Peter's story encourage you?

How might you respond if Jesus were to call you by name and ask you, "_____, do you love me?"

What do you think Jesus might ask you to do for him as a sign of your love?

Spend some time prayerfully considering how God has been calling you to care for his flock. What opportunities has God been opening up for you to pour into the lives of others and make the journey of faith with them?

DAY FOUR: Life to the Fullest

As you've been reading John's Gospel, you may have noticed the frequent use of the word *life*. It appears more in this Gospel than in any other book in the New Testament. In fact, more than one fourth of all the mentions of *life* in the New Testament are found in John's Gospel.

1. Look up the passages in the chart on the next page. What does each reveal about the "life" John's Gospel mentions?

Scripture	What this passage reveals about "life"
John 1:4	
John 3:16	
John 3:36	
John 5:21	
John 5:40	
John 6:35	
John 6:63	
John 8:12	
John 10:10	
John 10:17	
John 20:31	

These passages demonstrate that a relationship with Christ is the source of all life. In what ways have you discovered this to be true?

2. In what ways have you looked for life, including abundant life, outside of Jesus? What has been the result?

3. What spiritual practices strengthen your relationship with Jesus and awaken you spiritually?

4. Which areas of your life would you like to fill so that you're overflowing with God's presence and abundant life?

Spend some time asking Jesus to fill you with himself, his presence, his promise of life. Ask Jesus to reveal himself to you in a fresh way so that you're overflowing with joyful, abundant life.

DAY FIVE: Reflecting on God's Beauty in John's Gospel

After engaging in a Bible study, sometimes it's easy to move on to the next one without taking time to reflect on what God has been communicating to you. Like a traveler on a long road trip, you can wake up and wonder, "Where have I just been?"

1. Spend a few moments flipping through the pages of your participant's guide. Which statements or notes did you underline or highlight?

Why were these meaningful to you?

2. What did you learn through this study that you'd never known before about John's Gospel?

How do these insights impact your relationship with Jesus?

3. Where have you seen the beauty of God most clearly on display in the Gospel of John?

4. Why is it important to continue pursuing God's beauty in your own life? As you reflect on the stories of Jesus communicated through John's Gospel, where did you see the beauty of God on display?

> **Quotable**
>
> "John's Gospel has rightly been called 'a Gospel of decision.' Every person must choose between light and darkness, faith or unbelief, life or death. Light, life, and salvation, in turn, can be attained only by faith in the crucified and risen Messiah, Jesus."[20]
>
> —Andreas J. Kostenberger

5. The purpose of John's Gospel is to move people toward a robust belief in Jesus Christ. In what ways has your own faith in Jesus been strengthened through this study?

Spend some time thanking God for all that you've learned and discovered through this study about God and his beautiful presence in our world. Ask God for the grace not only to see the beauty of God but also to reflect it in your everyday life.

Notes

1. *http://www.sermonsfromseattle.com/series_a_the_beauty_of_god.htm.*
2. Michael Card, *The Parable of Joy* (Nashville: Thomas Nelson, 1996), xxi.
3. Many thanks to my dear pastor friend Bill McCready, who responded with this insight in an email on 12/30/10.
4. Leon Morris, *The Gospel According to John: The New International Commentary on the New Testament* (Grand Rapids: Wm. B. Eerdmans, 1971), 254.
5. Gary Burge, *The NIV Application Commentary: John* (Grand Rapids: Zondervan, 2000), 226–227.
6. Jonathan Edwards, *A Treatise Concerning Religious Affections* (reprinted on lulu.com, 2007), 102.
7. *http://dictionary.reference.com/browse/blind+spots.*
8. Morris, 94.
9. St. Irenaeus, *Against Heresies*, IV, 6:6.
10. Anthony Coniaris, *Do Something Beautiful for God* (Minneapolis: Light and Life Press, 2006), 85.
11. Paul Louis Metzger, *The Gospel of John: When Love Comes to Town* (Downers Grove, Ill.: InterVarsity Press, 2010), 144.
12. *http://dictionary.reference.com/browse/abide.*
13. Richard Harries, *Art and the Beauty of God: A Christian Understanding* (New York: Mowbray, 1993), 6.
14. William Barclay, *The Gospel of John*, New Daily Study Bible, vol. 2 (Louisville: Westminster John Knox Press, 2001), 231.
15. Morris, 766.
16. N. T. Wright, *Simply Christian: Why Christianity Makes Sense* (San Francisco: HarperOne, 2006), 47.
17. Max Lucado, *The Gospel of John* (Nashville: Thomas Nelson, 2006), 106.
18. Craig R. Koester, *Symbolism in the Fourth Gospel: Meaning, Mystery, Community* (Minneapolis: Fortress Press, 2003), 288.
19. Koester, 121.
20. Andreas J. Kostenberger, *Zondervan Illustrated Bible Backgrounds Commentary: John* (Grand Rapids: Zondervan, 2002), 4.

Bibliography

Bailey, Kenneth E. *Jesus through Middle Eastern Eyes: Cultural Studies in the Gospels.* Downers Grove, Ill.: InterVarsity Press, 2008.

Blackaby, Henry, Richard Blackaby, Thomas Blackaby, Melvin Blackaby, and Norman Blackaby. *Encounters with God: John, Small Group Study.* Nashville: Thomas Nelson, 2007.

Blomberg, Craig L. *The Historical Reliability of the Gospels,* second ed. Downers Grove, Ill.: InterVarsity Press, 2007.

Blomberg, Craig L. *Preaching the Parables: From Responsible Interpretation to Powerful Proclamation.* Grand Rapids: Baker, 2004.

Brown, Raymond E. *The Gospel According to John XII-XXI: A New Translation with Introduction and Commentary.* Vol. 29A. New Haven: Yale University Press, 1970.

Burge, Gary M. *The NIV Application Commentary: John.* Grand Rapids: Zondervan, 2000.

Card, Michael. *The Parable of Joy.* Nashville: Thomas Nelson, 1995.

Connelly, Douglas. *John: The Way to True Life.* Downers Grove, Ill.: InterVarsity Press, 2002.

Fredrikson, Roger L. *The Communicator's Commentary: John.* Waco, Texas: Word, 1985.

Koester, Craig R. *Symbolism in the Fourth Gospel: Meaning, Mystery, Community,* second ed. Minneapolis: Fortress Press, 2003.

Kostenberger, Andreas J. *Zondervan Illustrated Bible Backgrounds Commentary: John.* Grand Rapids: Zondervan, 2002.

The Learning Bible (Contemporary English Version). New York: American Bible Society, 2000.

Longman III, Tremper and David E. Garland, eds. *The Expository Bible Commentary: Luke–Acts,* rev. ed. Vol. 10. Grand Rapids: Zondervan, 2007.

Lucado, Max. *The Gospel of John.* Nashville: Thomas Nelson, 2006.

MacArthur, John. *John: Jesus—the Word, the Messiah, the Son of God.* Nashville: Thomas Nelson, 2007.

Matson, Mark A. *Interpretation Bible Studies: John.* Louisville: Westminster John Knox Press, 2002.

Metzger, Paul Louis. *The Gospel of John: When Love Comes to Town.* Downers Grove, Ill.: InterVarsity Press, 2010.

Sloyan, Gerard S. *John: Interpretation, a Bible Commentary for Teaching and Preaching.* Atlanta: John Knox Press, 1988.

Swindoll, Charles R. *Swindoll's New Testament Insights: John.* Grand Rapids: Zondervan, 2010.

About the Author

A popular speaker at churches and leading conferences such as Catalyst and Thrive, Margaret Feinberg was recently named one of the "30 Emerging Voices" who will help lead the church in the next decade by *Charisma* magazine and one of the "40 Under 40" who will shape Christian publishing by *Christian Retailing*. She has written more than two dozen books and Bible studies including the critically-acclaimed *The Organic God, The Sacred Echo, Scouting the Divine* (Zondervan) and their corresponding DVD Bible studies. She is known for her relational teaching style and for inviting people to discover the relevance of God and the Scriptures in a modern world.

Margaret and her books have been covered by national media including: CNN, the Associated Press, *Los Angeles Times, Dallas Morning News, Washington Post, Chicago Tribune, Newsday, Houston Chronicle,* Beliefnet.com, Salon.com, USATODAY.com, MSNBC.com, RealClearPolitics.com, Forbes.com, and many others.

Margaret currently lives in Colorado with her 6'8" husband, Leif. When she's not writing or traveling, she enjoys anything outdoors, lots of laughter, and their superpup, Hershey. But she says some of her best moments are spent communicating with her readers. So go ahead, drop her a note:

Margaret Feinberg
P.O. Box 441
Morrison, CO 80465

www.margaretfeinberg.com
info@margaretfeinberg.com

"Like" on Facebook
Follow on Twitter: *@mafeinberg*

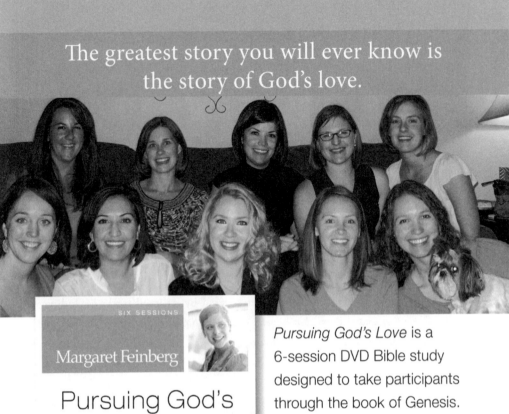

margaretfeinberg.com

Great Resources for You and Your Small Group
at www.margaretfeinberg.com

On the site, you'll find:

-Weekly giveaways
-Free e-newsletter sign-up
-Margaret's personal blog
-Interactive discussion board

-Video and audio clips
-Secret sales and promotions
-Travel schedule
-Great prices on Bible studies

 become a fan on facebook
facebook.com/margaretfeinberg

 become a twitter follower
@mafeinberg

Share Your Thoughts

With the Author: Your comments will be forwarded to the author when you send them to *zauthor@zondervan.com*.

With Zondervan: Submit your review of this book by writing to *zreview@zondervan.com*.

Free Online Resources at
www.zondervan.com

Zondervan AuthorTracker: Be notified whenever your favorite authors publish new books, go on tour, or post an update about what's happening in their lives at www.zondervan.com/authortracker.

Daily Bible Verses and Devotions: Enrich your life with daily Bible verses or devotions that help you start every morning focused on God. Visit www.zondervan.com/newsletters.

Free Email Publications: Sign up for newsletters on Christian living, academic resources, church ministry, fiction, children's resources, and more. Visit www.zondervan.com/newsletters.

Zondervan Bible Search: Find and compare Bible passages in a variety of translations at www.zondervanbiblesearch.com.

Other Benefits: Register yourself to receive online benefits like coupons and special offers, or to participate in research.

ZONDERVAN.com/
AUTHORTRACKER
follow your favorite authors